Citizenship as a Challenge

AF714625

At the Interface/Probing the Boundaries

Founding Editor

Rob Fisher (*Progressive Connexions*)

Advisory Board

Peter Bray (*University of Auckland*)
Robert Butler (*Elmhurst College*)
Ioana Cartarescu (*Independent Scholar*)
Seán Moran (*Waterford Institute of Technology*)
Stephen Morris (*Independent Scholar*)
John Parry (*Lewis & Clark College*)
Natalia Kaloh Vid (*University of Maribor*)

VOLUME 136

The titles published in this series are listed at *brill.com/aipb*

Citizenship as a Challenge

Dimensions of an Evolving Process

Edited by

Tamara Nair and Maria Inês Amaro

BRILL

LEIDEN | BOSTON

Cover illustration: Crowd at a party, photograph by Mario Purisic, image provided via unsplash.com.

Library of Congress Cataloging-in-Publication Data

Names: Becoming a Citizen (Conference) (2015 Mansfield College, University of Oxford) | Nair, Tamara, editor. | Amaro, Maria Inês, editor.
Title: Citizenship as a challenge : dimensions of an evolving process / edited by Tamara Nair, Maria Inês Amaro.
Description: Leiden ; Boston : Brill Nijhoff, [2022] | Series: At the interface/probing the boundaries, 1570-7113 ; volume 136 | Includes bibliographical references and index.
Identifiers: LCCN 2021043488 (print) | LCCN 2021043489 (ebook) | ISBN 9789004429246 (paperback) | ISBN 9789004429253 (ebook)
Subjects: LCSH: Citizenship–Congresses. | Citizenship–Social aspects–Congresses. | LCGFT: Conference papers and proceedings.
Classification: LCC K3224.A6 B43 2022 (print) | LCC K3224.A6 (ebook) | DDC 342.08/3–dc23/eng/20211004
LC record available at https://lccn.loc.gov/2021043488
LC ebook record available at https://lccn.loc.gov/2021043489

Typeface for the Latin, Greek, and Cyrillic scripts: "Brill". See and download: brill.com/brill-typeface.

ISSN 1570-7113
ISBN 978-90-04-42924-6 (paperback)
ISBN 978-90-04-42925-3 (e-book)

Copyright 2022 by Koninklijke Brill NV, Leiden, The Netherlands.
Koninklijke Brill NV incorporates the imprints Brill, Brill Nijhoff, Brill Hotei, Brill Schöningh, Brill Fink, Brill mentis, Vandenhoeck & Ruprecht, Böhlau Verlag and V&R Unipress.
All rights reserved. No part of this publication may be reproduced, translated, stored in a retrieval system, or transmitted in any form or by any means, electronic, mechanical, photocopying, recording or otherwise, without prior written permission from the publisher. Requests for re-use and/or translations must be addressed to Koninklijke Brill NV via brill.com or copyright.com.

This book is printed on acid-free paper and produced in a sustainable manner.

Contents

Notes on Contributors

Maria Inês Amaro
PhD, Social Work, is an Assistant Professor at the University Institute of Lisbon (ISCTE-IUL) and

Francisco Branco
PhD, Social Work, is an Associate Professor at the Catholic University of Portugal.

Amanda Bigler
PhD, School of Arts, English and Drama, Loughborough University, UK. Amanda is currently an English lecturer and researcher at Université de Lilli 3, France.

Y.Y. Brandon Chen
is an Assistant Professor at the University of Ottawa, Faculty of Law (Common Law Section). His current research examines health and social inequities that arise in the context of international migration.

Philippa Hunter
PhD, is a Senior Lecturer in history and social sciences education, and curriculum studies at the School of Education-Te Kura Toi Tangata, University of Waikato, New Zealand. Her research interests include history and social sciences curriculum in initial teacher education, narrative research of problematised history pedagogy, and evidence-based inquiry across curricula.

Tamara Nair
PhD, Development Studies, is a Research Fellow at the S. Rajaratnam School of International Studies, in Nanyang Technological University (NTU), Singapore. Her research interests include human security and human development.

Paula Leal Tejeda
PhD, Education. University of Sussex. CONICYT Chile, Beca de Doctorado en el Extranjero, 72100582. Paula is currently a Lecturer in Universidad Autónoma de Chile, Temuco.

S. Ram Vemuri
is an Economist currently working as an Associate Professor of Economics at Charles Darwin University, Darwin, Northern Territory, Australia. He has written extensively on economics, diasporas, pluralism and the interaction of multiculturalism and ethics.

Judith Zangerle
PhD, herself is a 'global nomad', holding an Italian passport, belonging to a German speaking minority in the heart of the Alps, married to a North African, crossing borders and continents frequently. She received her teaching degree in Austria and completed her PhD in Intercultural Linguistics at the Universidad de Cádiz (Spain) in June 2019. Currently, she is back teaching at a secondary school for nursery education in Austria after one year of maternity leave.

Lana Zdravković
PhD, Philosophy, is a researcher, political activist, publicist and performance artist. Her research interests include identity, citizenship, migrations, political engagement, radical equality and politics of emancipation.

Being a Citizen

Tamara Nair and Maria Inês Amaro

This edited volume is a result of a conference, "Becoming a Citizen" by Interdisciplinary.Net – a global network for research and publishing – held at Mansfield College, Oxford, United Kingdom from Saturday 11th July – Monday 13th July 2015. This was part of ID.Net's Third Global Meeting in the Citizenship Project. Unfortunately, ID. Net has since shut down its operations, but it was felt that the papers presented at the conference deserved greater exposure, especially in light of the tumultuous events happening in the world from when we started talking about the topic of citizenship to the various ways it is being experienced or expressed now.

Citizenship is one of the most important legacies of human development. It raises the human status from a biological condition into a cultural, moral, political and rationalistic one. This is an open-ended process, constantly evolving and, with each new turn, adding complexity to human existence.

Being a citizen not only implies a process of recognition but also the development of a system of protection. In other words, citizenship relates to a process of acknowledging the human status as unique, but it also addresses a quest for rights and duties, with political, governmental, legal, ethical, economic, and social dimensions attached.

After the breakthroughs of the eighteenth century, with the first steps in recognition of civil and political rights, and of the twentieth century with the advancement of social rights and the emergence of cultural and environmental rights, one could be led to the conclusion that the twenty-first century would see more of a consolidation and enlargement of citizenship ideas and ideals.

On the contrary, contemporary times have proven to be surprisingly challenging for the idea of citizenship. The increasing influence of a xenophobic political discourse, the refugee crisis, the re-emergence of nationalism(s), the weakening of democratic decision-making processes, the austerity policies, the outbreak of war in civil urban contexts, the sustainability menace, the uncertainty about news, facts and the truth, the generalised climate of suspicion; all these, interlinked or otherwise, are factors of a scenario of disruption, which puts the ideas and the boundaries of citizenship in jeopardy.

More immediately, it is possible to clearly identify attacks on social rights. However, political and civil rights are increasingly suffering multiple threats on a day-to-day basis as well, even in geo-political contexts that used to be taken as the example to follow, as the case of Europe demonstrates.

© KONINKLIJKE BRILL NV, LEIDEN, 2022 | DOI:10.1163/9789004429253_002

The present book was written while some significant events were happening in the world. Indeed, the past few years were abundant in political, social, military facts which imply multiple tensions into the realisation of citizenship. Hence, this book aims at reflecting and discussing citizenship from various points of view and academic disciplines. It is organised in four different sections, according to the different approaches to citizenship proposed by the contributors. Contributions come from different fields ranging from Literature and Cultural Studies to Philosophy, Political Science, Law, Sociology and Social Work.

Part 1 is an overture chapter, with some conceptual and more abstract discussions about the topic. In this chapter, Ram Vemuri discusses the 'shopping of citizenship' where an individual exercises choice of where to belong, which raises concerns of where individual allegiance lies. Against this backdrop, Vemuri examines the roles and responsibilities of citizenship and the presence of an unconscious bias that colours contemporary citizenship discourse.

Part 2 explores the administrative dimensions of citizenship, with the State appearing as a central actor in protecting the 'values' of citizenship. Chapters here, each in its own way, discuss policies that effectuate or hinder respect for citizenship. Starting us off in examining the role of the State, the chapter by Amaro and Branco argues how the adoption of a minimum protection policy or a normative and civilizational reference is required to safeguard the fundamental rights of citizenship. Based on their study on Minimum Income Standard in Portugal, the authors analyse citizens' rationalities when discussing what one should possess to attain an adequate standard of living in Portugal.

From another angle on administrative rationalism, the chapter by Y.Y. Brandon Chen studies the case of international migrants and public healthcare in Canada. Chen argues that the exclusionary propensity of Canadian citizenship is sometimes reined in by inclusionary norms to even enable the entry of migrants to be seen as undesirable because of their suspected dependence on public healthcare. According to Chen, this has resulted in particularistic welfare controls that query foreign residents' labour market contributions and the genuineness of their humanitarian needs.

Amanda Bigler's unique contribution assessing the role of the State in defining citizenship is revealed through a creative non-fictional account of being detained and subsequently deported from Heathrow Airport in London. Bigler's writing explores the stringent and contradictory practices of the United Kingdom Border Agency (UKBA). The author presents a first-hand account of the UKBA detention, its centres and its practices.

Moving on, Part 3 develops the debate on education for citizenship, working on issues of citizenship arising within school settings or amongst young people. It also problematizes the cultural challenges faced by youth in dealing with their own diversity in terms of national and cultural references. The first, Philippa Hunter's chapter on representations of young citizens in New Zealand's schooling curriculum, questions if young people are compliant, standardised or agentive citizens in the making. From a critical pedagogy stance, Hunter examines ways in which New Zealand's curriculum policy-shaping strategies conceptualise young citizens in the making across 13 years of primary and secondary school education. More importantly, Hunter's chapter enquires how curriculum spaces and possibilities rethink citizenship and future-oriented narratives of representation.

With renewed interests in citizenship in both international and national education contexts, Paula Leal's chapter discusses several reforms in education in Chile, led by various governments since the return to democracy in 1990, after Augusto Pinochet's dictatorship. Leal highlights insights into what secondary school students understand by citizenship and citizenship education in Chile and how the education system, through the curriculum and schools, influence those understandings.

Concluding the section is Judith Zangerle's examination of 'Third Culture Kids' and their experiences in today's mobile and highly globalised world. Zangerle's chapter highlights the invisible struggles of these 'Third Culture Kids' who increasingly experience a confused sense of identity due to personal histories, which often involve transitions, grief and struggles to fit in. She reminds us that these 'new' global citizens are on the rise and should therefore not be overlooked in studies that examine the meaning of being a citizen.

And in concluding this collection, Part 4 explores 'models' of governance for citizenship and how this concept might be approached as organised action towards rights recognition and protection. Tamara Nair's chapter focuses on how citizenship governance has altered ideas of rights and freedoms, using the state of Kerala in South India as a case study. In examining reservation seats that mandate political rights to India's marginalised communities, Nair argues that ideas of citizenship are centred on the bodies of the marginalised in society and fail to represent individual rights and freedoms that citizenship encompasses.

Alternatively, Lana Zdravković's chapter, *Inventing Citizenship*, criticises the nation-state's actions that reduces citizenship into membership of a national community. In the style of Arendt, Balibar and Habermas, Zdravković argues that citizenship is a political concept and should move beyond the private activity of maximising happiness. It is a communicative engagement of active people working within the processes and activities that defines citizenship.

If not by other reasons, the various chapters presented in this collection and the current state of the world points out very emphatically the importance of not letting go and of furthering the debates and reflections about citizenship. We argue that citizenship should not be viewed as a taken for granted concept, but as one that needs to be re-discussed and conquered on a daily basis.

The diverse contributions in this book are also evidence of the multidisciplinary character of the topic, which seems to be regarded as timely by various and different academic disciplines.

At this juncture, we would like to thank all the authors who contributed to this volume and thank them especially for their patience with the whole publishing process. We would also especially like to acknowledge the work of Amanda Bigler who was greatly involved in the initial editorial phase. We tried many instances to contact Amanda to gain her formal permission for the publication of her chapter. Unfortunately, we were unable to. However, given that Amanda has made an initial submission for publication and has informally agreed to publish, we have taken the liberty to include her work. We feel her chapter adds depth to this collection and that readers will benefit from her writing.

It is our opinion that much of what is in this volume transcends the past five years and in fact should mould our thinking on what should constitute citizenship narratives moving forward.

Afterword, February 2021

This edited volume was supposed to be published towards the end of 2019 but unfortunately was moved a number of times. We hold ourselves responsible and stand guilty as charged. However, in our defence we have to add that this long delay was mostly a result of an unprecedented global experience – COVID-19.

The year 2020 has been quite a rollercoaster ride for us, as it has been for the world in general. We felt that this prolonged delay and with many of us in our homes, struggling to manage our work and lives within the same space and time, may have, unfortunately or fortunately, provided us with an opportunity to review some of our initial thoughts around this volume (we believe *the glass is half-full!*). It seemed to us that there are many evolving ideas of citizenship, in the years since our Conference in Mansfield College in Oxford, that found magnification this year.

We have touched upon some of these ideas early in this introduction when we talked about contemporary times and how ideas of citizenship have evolved around the increasing influence of populism, the mass movement of people across the globe, the re-emergence of nationalism(s), especially during this pandemic; related to that, the disturbing impacts of austerity policies, the continued questionable credibility of news, facts and the now infamous 'alternative facts', and the most recent developments that have spread – *#MeToo!* and *Black Lives Matter* movements, both of which have done their rounds around the world. These 'events' have called for a cross-examination of the ideas and boundaries of citizenship.

The genesis of the Trump administration on January 20, 2016, re-evaluated what it meant to be a citizen not only in the United States of America, but by virtue of the power of the US President, how citizenship was redefined under the influence of his administration. Although not a direct correlation to the Trump presidency, we have seen similar strongmen appear or 'reappear' as the case may be, around the world. From Rodrigo Duterte in the Philippines and issues of extra judiciary killings and human rights violations that mire his administration,[1] to Jair Bolsanaro in Brazil[2] and Nicolás Maduro in Venezuela,[3] both seemingly ignoring large sections of their citizens and their plights under their leadership, to Marine le Pen in France, stoking the fires of anti-globalization,[4] to Uganda's long-term leader Yoweri Museveni arresting opposition presidential hopeful, Ugandan Reggae singer, Bobi Wine, before a rally because he was popular and standing against him,[5] to Mohammad bin Salman of Saudi Arabia, supposed liberator of women/jailer of female activists,[6] and implicated in the murder of Saudi national and journalist Jamal Khashoggi,[7] and to Xi Jinping

1 Santos, Ana, P. "Duterte's four years in power – extrajudicial killings, rights abuses and terror." 7 July 2020. *Deutsche Welle*. https://www.dw.com/en/dutertes-four-years-in-power-extrajudicial-killings-rights-abuses-and-terror/a-54082293.

2 Rachman, Gideon. "Jair Bolsonaro's populism is leading Brazil to disaster." *The Financial Times*. 25 May 2020. https://www.ft.com/content/c39fadfe-9e60-11ea-b65d-489c67b0d85d.

3 BBC News. "Venezuela crisis: How the political situation escalated." 3 December 2020. https://www.bbc.com/news/world-latin-america-36319877.

4 Reuters. "Le Pen says will defend France against globalization." 24 April 2017. https://www.reuters.com/article/us-france-election-le-pen-idUSKBN17P0TW.

5 Al Jazeera. "Bobi Wine 'beaten' by Ugandan police after presidential nomination." 3 November 2020. https://www.aljazeera.com/news/2020/11/3/bobi-wine-uganda-presidential-poll-candidate-arrested-party.

6 Kalin, Stephen and Summer Said. "Saudi Women's Rights Activist Sentenced to Nearly Six Years in Prison." *The Wall Street Journal*. 28 December 2020. https://www.wsj.com/articles/saudi-womens-rights-activist-convicted-by-terrorism-court-11609168687.

7 DeYoung, Karen. "Saudi crown prince approved operation that led to death of journalist Jamal Kashoggi, US intelligence report concludes." *The Washington Post*. 27 February 2021. https://www.washingtonpost.com/national-security/khashoggi-killing-intelligence-report-release-mbs-saudi-arabia/2021/02/26/df5f6e58-7844-11eb-948d-19472e683521_story.html.

and the alleged treatment of Uighurs and their 're-education' in Xinjiang province in China.[8] From here we see how the idea of citizenship is more than just belonging to a particular nation and enjoying the rights it accords. Citizenship is pegged to almost anything, from your race and ethnicity, your class, your gender, your freedom to oppose what you feel is flawed leadership, your ties to the land as an indigenous community, and finally to the very principles you hold dear and believe in deeply. Nothing exemplifies the latter better than the case of Muslims in India.

Indian Prime Minister, Narendra Modi's, Bharatiya Janata Party's new Citizenship Amendment Act of 2019 allegedly utilises religion as a condition for deciding whether illegal migrants in India can be advanced for citizenship.[9] The bill that favours members of all South Asia's major religions, except Islam, has raised red flags and protests across India's 200-million-strong Muslim community – the world's largest Muslim-minority population. It has also gathered condemnation from other communities in India including its majority Hindu population. Many have called it for what it is, blatant discrimination of a particular religious group. The bill touches the very heart of what it means to be a citizen in the world's largest democracy. We start to question then, where do India's 200 million Muslims citizens stand where the ruling party is concerned?

From the world's largest democracy to the world's oldest; the idea of race and citizenship has been laid bare with the death of George Floyd in Minneapolis on May 25, 2020, triggering a massive snowballing of grief and anger not only in the US but also around the world. The idea of a large community of people who have always felt themselves to be 'second class' citizens in their own country and their different lives against the much admired "American Dream" lifestyle has been represented in US through popular culture, the arts, music and literature and of course in the lived experiences of African Americans as reported in the media. But these feelings of oppression and injustice came to a head with the death of George Floyd in the hands of the police – an arm of the State meant to protect and serve its citizens. Not only did Floyd's death spark major unrest in the streets of US but galvanised protestors around issues of discrimination and injustice perpetrated against minority groups, mostly of African and Asian heritage, in countries across the Atlantic and across the world. Deep-seated unhappiness and anger over decades of discrimination

---

8 Ramzy, Austin and Chris Buckley. "Absolutely No Mercy: Leaked Files Expose How China Organized Mass Detention of Muslims". *The New York Times*. 16 November 2019. https://www.nytimes.com/interactive/2019/11/16/world/asia/china-xinjiang-documents.html.

9 BBC News. "India protests: PM Modi defends citizenship bill amid clashes." 22 December 2019. https://www.bbc.com/news/world-asia-india-50883819.

based on race and skin colour has overflown and registered as a re-learning and re-writing of history along with the 'evils' of colonialism – not only in the US but in former colonies, many of whose citizens still bear the scars of this segregation between coloniser and colonised.

Globalization certainly presented a renewed interest in the citizen and with what global events we have seen since this book project took off and are still seeing now; it would not be wrong of us to seriously question ideas of liberalism and the fundamental beliefs of liberal states or the idea of a social contract between citizen and the State. What does it mean to be a citizen? Are our rights as citizens dependent on race, gender, ethnicity or religion? Have we collectively assumed the 'us' versus 'them' narrative within our own borders, embracing a more insular stand?

We have seen these questions dig in and take root in COVID-19 times. Not only has the pandemic revealed the extent of interconnectedness of peoples and States, but it has also revealed the hierarchies of relationships between citizens and the State. Different economic classes, indigenous communities, marginalized groups for example, the LGBTQI community, have all had different experiences during the pandemic and this is a direct correlation between their communities, their rights as citizens and how society and the State continue to view them, contain them and work with them.

Despite these many global events that have reshaped ideas and identities of the citizen, we conclude with the assertion that all of our initial papers continue to resonate with current discussions around citizenship and what it means to be a citizen today. Our collection has merely provided an appetiser for the serious scholar studying citizenship. We hope the chapters presented here will be stepping stones to further research and study in the field. We humbly present it here to our readers.

In conclusion, we would like to extend our profound gratitude (and a heartfelt apology) to all our fantastic authors who have been extremely patient with us and the whole publishing process. They have been more than kind by tempering their expectations and allowing us the time to carve out the much-needed mental space to analyse all these new global developments that we have humbly attempted to put into words here. We would also like to thank our editors from Brill (it has been a long process), who have been nothing but patient with us throughout this time.

T. Nair
M.I. Amaro
February 2021

PART 1

Citizenship as a Global Asset

The Unconscious Bias in Silences of Global Citizenship

S. Ram Vemuri

Abstract

Global migration data suggests that one in five people currently live in a place other than that of their birth. In addition, naturalisation data reveals that many are becoming citizens of the 'adopted' countries. There is also evidence that many naturalised citizens are becoming return migrants. This has resulted in shopping for citizenship where one is pursuing choices to achieve best returns. In recent times, more individuals are exercising citizenship choices – choices of where to belong – more than ever before resulting in a fluid nature of the ebb and flow of citizenship. This type of development is impacting many areas of the modern state, raising real concerns about where individual allegiances lie. Against such a backdrop, this chapter examines the roles and responsibilities of citizenship. The chapter suggests the importance of recognising the existence of silence in the discourse on citizenship. The chapter calls for a simultaneous examination of the impacts of silence as well as the influence of unconscious bias in contemporary citizenship discussion.

Keywords

silence – multiple identities – security – citizenship duties – unconscious bias – constrained choices

1 Introduction[1]

This chapter is concerned with the impacts of contemporary trends in the global village we live in. People and capital, the two most important factors of production, are on the move in an unprecedented manner. For example, the study on world migration provides evidence that globally, one in five people

1 UN-DESA and OECD, 'World Migration in Figures' (2013), http://www.oecd.org/els/mig/World-Migration-in-Figures.pdf Viewed 5 May, 2015.

© KONINKLIJKE BRILL NV, LEIDEN, 2022 | DOI:10.1163/9789004429253_003

live in a place other than that of their birth.[1] There is overwhelming evidence of a recent and growing trend amongst migrants applying for naturalised citizenships.[2]

Migrants, in the not too distant past, were reluctant to become citizens of another country. Part of the reason was the policies of the country of birth that required them to forego their birth rights of citizenship if they chose to become citizens of another country. Trends in modern globalization and financial pressures by nation states changed citizenship policies, resulting in national and political boundaries being contested. These contestations are a result of a phenomenon that occurred around 30 years back amongst the migrants who relinquished their citizenship rights and duties of the place of their birth and took up citizenship in a foreign land. There is evidence of continuity of this phenomenon despite the challenges posed by *integration, identity and citizenship* in pluralistic and multicultural societies despite, and in some cases because of, an increase in the second and third generation migrants.[3]

The tensions resulting from economic, social, cultural, political and religious differences amongst multi-ethnic, multicultural populations have created ethnic enclaves (*bubbles*) producing *multiple identities* and *citizenships*. Therefore, in most nations of the world, issues related to migration and citizenship matter in an unprecedented manner than before.

'It is becoming obvious that migration does matter to all of us'.[4] It is because the increased global world is thronged by contesting boundaries in every aspect of life. The meaning assigned to citizenship is also affected by high levels of migration and increase in number of people choosing to take up citizenships. Citizenship itself is becoming a subject of investigation as there is a new emerging trend, targeting the *best deals* one can obtain from being a citizen of a land. This is referred to in this chapter as *citizenship shopping*.

Neither migration nor citizenship issues are new phenomena. However, the concern with citizenship shopping is the move away from terminological and

> … conceptual differences in the use of the idea of citizenship. It means different things to different people not in the least because of the

2 Elizabeth M. Grieco, et al., 'The Size, Place of Birth, and Geographic Distribution of the Foreign-Born Population in the United States: 1960 to 2010', U.S. Census Bureau, *Population Division Working Paper* 96 (2012):3. http://www.census.gov/population/foreign/files/WorkingPaper96.pdf Viewed 6 May, 2015.

3 Dina Mansour and Andrew Milne, *Negotiating Boundaries in Multicultural Societies* (Oxford: Inter-Disciplinary Press, 2014).

4 Mahni Dugan and Arnon Edelstein, *Migration Matters* (Oxford: Inter-Disciplinary Press, 2013).

> radical (also conservative) rethinking to which the idea of citizenship has recently been a subject.
>
> HEATER 1991, ROCHE 1992[5]

Until the 1990's, citizenship was considered an anchor for the individual to belong to a nation that formulates and later assumes similar values and traits in relation to tolerance, fair procedures, and respect for others belonging to the nation state; in short, discussions revolved around contributing to the 'very axis of society'[6] to which an individual belongs.

Citizenship was generally conceptualised in three ways: (1) a legal status or membership in a nation-state; (2) political, civil, social, and further rights and obligations; and (3) civic virtues.[7] However, in the recent human migration phase, the meaning ascribed to citizenship has become more confined to rights. It is therefore not a surprise that the discourse has moved to a framework involving deliberations about national citizenship rights and universal human rights. This is as long as individuals have a legal status and have contributed in some way to civic virtues. Invariably the contribution to civic virtues is through money creation and contribution to the exchequer. The focus of concern about citizenship has shifted dramatically.

Citizenship 'can be perceived of as a relationship between the state and individuals which gains its legitimacy because people 'believe' that certain rights will be obtained because people have 'deserved' these rights by obeying certain duties.'[8] Unfortunately such a transition from formation of citizenship values to human and universal citizenship rights has created two sets of anxieties in the communities across the world.

> One is the fear that, individually and collectively, we are losing control of the forces that govern our lives. The other is the sense that, from family to neighbourhood to nation, the moral fabric of community is unravelling

5 Susan J. Smith, 'Comment: Citizenship: All or Nothing?', *Political Geography* 14:2 (1995): 190–193.

6 Michael J. Sandel, *Democracy's Discontent: America in Search of a Public Philosophy* (Cambridge: The Belknap Press of Harvard University Press, 1996), 170.

7 Xiaobei Chen, 'The Child-Citizen, in Recasting the Social in Citizenship', *Recasting the Social in Citizenship*, cited by Engin F. Isin (Toronto: University of Toronto Press, 2008) as quoted in Synnove K.N. Bendixsen, 'Becoming Members of the Community of Value: Ethiopean Irregular Migrants Enacting Citizenship in Norway', in Dugan and Edelstein, *Migration Matters*, 7.

8 Kristoffer Halvorsrud, 'Negotiating the Economic Duties of Citizenship: White South Africans in the UK and Belonging Through 'Hard Work'', in Mansour and Milne, *Negotiating Boundaries in Multicultural Societies*, 9.

> around us. These two fears – for the loss of self-government and the erosion of community- together define the anxiety of age.[9]

A further anxiety has crept into the psyche of the individual and the nation. This relates to security and allegiance to national interests. Examining the reasons for such anxieties and related influences at the individual and societal levels invariably leads to recognising several actions shrouded in silence.

This chapter attempts to address the silences of global citizenships and suggests that an effective way to pursue and address these anxieties is to recognise both individual and government unconscious biases. The production of a dual and global citizen has become problematic in creating a framework that engages with the reality of nations and forces an investigation of the multicultural, multi-ethnic fabric of human geography in the contemporary nation state. It is in this context that we need to consider the unconscious bias when understanding silence in global citizenship discourse.

The chapter is organized as follows; First, the chapter attempts to provide a brief understanding of challenges of citizenship in a multicultural, multiethnic global world. The second part of the chapter combines three perspectives – the institutional, utilitarian and pluralistic- to explain why global citizenship has become the norm in contemporary societies. The third part of the chapter alludes to the existence of silence that is ever present in interactions amongst citizens in a contemporary context. The fourth part of the chapter suggests a need to recognise the prevalence of unconscious bias when dealing with silence related to global citizens. The chapter concludes with a call for a detailed examination of the unconscious bias in the silences of global citizenship to address contemporary challenges of today's modern state.

2 Understanding Citizenship

There are several challenges facing contemporary societies' understanding of citizenship. The main challenge related to citizenship in a multicultural, multi-ethnic global world relates, at a conceptual level, to the way citizenship is viewed by the individual, the group and the society. The involvements of the individual who has been a citizen and is embedded in the society is different to the migrant who has opted to become a citizen. It is a formidable challenge,

---

9 Michael J. Sandel, *Democracy's Discontent: America in Search of a Public Philosophy* (Cambridge: The Belknap Press of Harvard University Press, 1996), 3.

especially in democracies, to examine issues of concern of all citizens without an all-inclusive and collective frame of reference, independent of judiciary. The underlying cause for such an angst is the pluralistic nature of the citizen in the modern-day context which invariably involves multiplicity of perceptions about notions of justice and rights of citizenship. This is further exacerbated when individuals treat citizenship as a voluntary choice to be made based on a public philosophy of contemporary liberalism that promotes respect *for people's freedom to choose.*

The decisions made by individuals in exercising choices are not completely free but are constrained by the policies of the nation states and individual experiences. In countries that allow dual citizenships, for instance, individuals are identified with reference to two nationalities. However, there is another emerging trend where one also observes an increase in hyphenated identities where the individual is described, by oneself or others, as belonging to a composite of nationalities.

The hyphenated individual is all too common these days because of coexistence of multicultural populations due to the perceptions of individuals themselves as well as the perception of the *other.* It is also associated with how individuals feel about themselves in the context of mixed embeddedness and how individuals are perceived by others who are more fully embedded. Hyphen is often used to reflect the duality of composition which is becoming more prominent in the real-world commentary about different ethnicities being embedded in one nation.

Adopting a utilitarian perspective, one observes an individual state of fluidity and choices related to places of origin and residences. The ever-increasing number of migrants belonging to a diaspora – the diasporans – engaged in formal and informal networks is an illustration of such a trend. These are individuals who migrate, become members of the diasporas, are disenchanted with migration decisions as they are unable to embed themselves in the host societies and then use their networks and connections to either locate themselves for productive reasons in both host and home countries or other countries where there are members of their diasporas.

Diasporas' role in the world economy is becoming increasingly vital as the number of people living and working away from their places of birth is on the rise. Diasporas use their networks in the home, host and third countries and mostly become visible, and sometimes invisible, at the same time influencing living conditions in a world of globalised plural cultures.[10] However, the reality

10 Brubaker Rogers, 'The 'diaspora' diaspora', *Ethnic and Racial Studies* 28:1 (2005): 1- 19.

is that these very societies are also witnessing an increase in social tension and pressure on government funded services. Government funds for example are increasingly being called upon to meet the growing needs of all citizens irrespective of when individuals become citizens, as most democracies are committed to meeting the universal service obligations[11] Often, one witnesses a backlash as citizens who access publicly funded programs, such as housing, education and unemployment benefits, are resented by those who believe they *are entitled* for being *embedded in contributing to their countries of citizenship*. There is a tension between those who are embedded in the societies and those who are new citizens. This results in people delinking from spaces of their residences and becoming global citizens with very little affinity to any one political-economic space. This is one of the many reasons why the concept of the Global village has emerged.

3 Understanding Global Citizenship

The reality of Global Citizenship is to experience the elusive nature of being a citizen of the world. The narrative experiences of many global citizens have been discussed in terms of a loss of spatial connections with ramifications for freedom, responsibility and privilege on the part of the individuals in different spaces. While these aspects are the same as citizenship issues, the manner and extent of influences are quite distinct. This is partly because citizens' experiences in economic, political, cultural, social, historical, literary works, the media and the like, often influence thinking. There is overwhelming impact on the emotional and psychological effects on individuals and groups in society through global citizen activities including international investments, conducting international business, production and marketing. In addition, global citizens are playing an influential role in areas as diverse as health, wellbeing, livelihoods in home and host countries. These global citizens are also influencing the viability of numerous new developments, ventures, and even act as bridge-builders in many aspects of human activity, including sponsorship of concerts, sports events, looking after their children and grand-children's needs through emotional, economic and financial contributions. All these activities come at a price.

11 UNCTAD, 'Report of the Expert Meeting on Universal Access to Services' (2006), http://unctad.org/Sections/wcmu/docs/c1em30p004_en.pdf Viewed 19 July 2018.

The human landscape in many nation states raises some very deep and fundamental questions as individual nations shift their attention to an *axis of a multicultural society* created through a rise in global citizenships. The underlying basis of 'daily practice, the assumptions about citizenship and freedom that inform public life'[12] is often reduced to a single point of reference, namely of treating individuals in contemporary societies as *equal right bearing agents.* The policy implications are far reaching.

> Laws are drafted from the perspective of the generalised other, which means that those who obey the law are automatically recognised by others who also obey the law. Having the backing of the law is necessary for development and maintenance of self-respect, since people are able to represent themselves only when they know that they deserve the respect of the others.[13]

Global citizens in contemporary societies recognise the significance of these laws. In negotiating their actions in ever changing political, social and economic landscapes through global interactions, one can witness a shift in behaviour where most global citizens abide by the laws of the nations because the 'right-bearers not only have equal access to welfare goods and liberties, but also enjoy the status of a full member(ship) of a political community'.[14] By virtue of being global citizens the right-bearers simultaneously contextualise themselves with both home and host communities.

Global citizens in pluralistic multicultural contemporary societies face challenges of boundary negotiation in the form of *belonging* and *exclusion*. The 'challenges of integration, identity and citizenship within multicultural societies'[15] *and their experiences* are 'creating a procedural framework of principles that governs human behaviour and allows many diverse ways of life to co-exist peacefully, without the presumption of overarching common values'.[16]

The procedural framework, sometimes referred to as a bureaucratic framework, although necessary, is woefully inadequate to address the issues of

12 Ibid.

13 Francis Levrau, 'Esteem and Respect in a Multicultural Society', in Dugan and Edelstein, *Migration Matters*, 169.

14 Ibid.

15 Mansour and Milne, *Negotiating Boundaries in Multicultural Societies* (Oxford: Inter-Disciplinary Press, 2014).

16 Francis Luong, 'Separating Illiberal from Liberal People', in Mansour and Milne *Negotiating Boundaries*, 93.

pluralism in modern contemporary societies as witnessed in daily observations. Unintentionally, the framework currently used has created two worlds – a world that absorbs citizens into the main frame and another that does not and ascribes a *minority status*. The former groups of citizens are individuals 'able to develop self- respect since they can consider themselves equally competent, free and autonomous deliberators. Conversely', the latter, the minority are 'people who lack self-respect feel less autonomy and the quality of their lives suffers as a result'.[17]

Even though the modern-state finds pluralism a goal, at the same time, it regards certain elements of pluralism as a threat. Communities are grappling with issues like how to deal with ISIS, the near-independence of Scotland, ongoing viability of the EU, Russia vs. Ukraine vs. international community and asylum-seekers, just to name a few. At the same time, the increased diversification of population due to large-scale immigrations, and celebration of diversity of populations in modern nation-states is imposing challenges on managing diversity.

Modern nation-states are grappling with a few core issues resulting from pursuing the pluralism goal. They include: (a) dealing with curtailment of individual freedoms amid fears of attack; (b) striking a balance between 'secrecy', police and the state surveillance, individual privacy, post wiki-leaks in a strong cyber-linked world; (c) planning cities and spaces and addressing ghettos of urban communities in "quarters" where tourists visit (such as the 'Arab quarter' in Paris, the 'Jewish quarter' in London, etc.); and (d) evaluating the impact and influence of ethnic groups on local economies, shop traders, etc.

The nation-state requires new modes of thought and analysis, as global trends in population, capital flows, cultural exchanges, cyber links and the like enmesh with post-national forces, challenging the stability of the nation-state and its permanence as the basic socio-political construct.

The new way of thinking must begin with an escape from promoting absorption of new migrants into the mainstream of society through a cycle of separation, alienation and marginalisation. Those people who are absorbers of the culture of places of domicile, the absorbers, suggest that the bureaucratic treatment of immigrants as *needy* people creates a mind-set amongst many of the civil servants that they are *entitled to interfere in the lives of immigrants, channel their connections, and adopt determining functions*, as they see fit. *Adopting a universal service delivery model sometimes* results 'in a disregard

17 Francis Levrau, 'Esteem and Respect in a Multicultural Society: A critical Analysis of Axel Hometh's Recognition Theory', in Dugan and Edelstein, *Migration Matters*, 169.

for the immigrants' culture of origin, a delay in their integration into the host society, and enhanced dependence on the absorbers'.[18]

The effect of the policies prescribed along these lines is challenging the very axis of society underpinning citizenship referred to earlier. For example, the debate about taking away citizenship status of those who are a threat to the safety and functioning of society in Australia is raising several questions about freedom, responsibility and privilege. The discussion is raising questions about the relationship between the individual and the society. Unfortunately, the discussion is often shrouded in 'silence' as there are several interpretations to the meanings assigned for citizenship. This is especially because of a lack of recognition and acknowledgement of the impact of silence and its modalities on citizenship in multicultural and pluralistic societies.

4 'Silences' in Global Citizenship

Silence in the discussion of citizenship is very minimal. Attention to silence is important for understanding the in-between space that is a dwelling place of a number of citizens in multicultural and pluralistic interactions. It is also important to recognise that when individual silences are broken, they are invariably past the stage of discussion and lack any links to others in mainstream society. Therefore, timely understanding and examination of how to incorporate silence into discussions concerning citizenship requires explicit attention. Part of the complexity is with the lack of discussion around the *axis of (contemporary) pluralistic societies*. Aggregating and representing individual units of analysis amongst persons, regions, and nations in relation to modern contemporary citizenship contexts is indeed a formidable challenge. What does it entail?

Attention to silence is crucial in forming the axis as referred to above. The disengagement of individuals is resulting in more people occupying the in-between spaces. One can observe this especially in contexts when decisions are made through the process of aggregation and representation in contemporary societies still engaging in public policy frameworks based on the social fabric of relatively stable populations. Over time even with marginal adjustments to decision making frameworks, these in-between spaces are increasingly being filled with silences as the non-mainstream voices are not heard and often not

18 Arnon Edelstein, 'Intimate Partner Femicide (IPF) Among Ethiopian Women in Israel', in Dugan and Edelstein, *Migration Matters*, 144–145.

even recognised that they exist. It is therefore of no surprise that references are made about the *silent majority*.

Recognising silence in citizenship interactions involves paying attention to several motivational factors for citizen engagement. It is also necessary to recognise that silence exists in citizenship discourse as one interpretation dominates. It is also important to interpret silence through an understanding of several modalities of silence. All these actions require one to move beyond oneself and one's view of citizenship. It requires a recognition of the unconscious bias in perception of what citizenship means.

The move beyond oneself *into the space between individuals in the society* involves a continual process of infusion and diffusion. In the former, the commencement and direction of the process moves in a direction from the individual to the group. The individual view of citizenship is projected onto the group. The latter is a movement from the group to the individual. It is through such explicit, conscious and deliberate attempts at examining both the infusion and diffusion processes that one understands citizenship interactions leading to a much-needed considerate view of the axis of the contemporary society.

5 Role of Unconscious Bias

In dealing with silences in the citizenship interactions through discourse analysis, modalities of silence need to be understood very carefully by differentiating between the infusion and diffusion processes of the perception of both the observer and the observed *other*.

It is also important to recognise that the way one perceives one another is conditioned by thought and perception. It is important to recognise the existence of conditioned learning in the way one perceives others and oneself.

The starting point in understanding the silences of global citizenship is through an acknowledgement that unconscious bias exists in all of us, including the analyst and the narrator. These are biases 'created and reinforced by our environments and experiences. Our mind is constantly processing information, often times without conscious awareness'[19] of our prejudices. If we are not cognizant of this altruism, we will not be satisfactorily addressing the issues of concern with global citizenships.

---

19 https:///www.gv.com/lib/unconcious-bias-at-work. Viewed 15 July 2015.

This chapter therefore calls for a detailed examination of the unconscious bias in silences of global citizenship to address contemporary challenges of the today's modern state.

Bibliography

Brubaker, Rogers, 'The 'diaspora' diaspora', Ethnic and Racial Studies 28:1 (2005): 1–19.

Chen, Xiaobei, 'The Child-Citizen, in Recasting the Social in Citizenship', *Recasting the Social in Citizenship*, by Engin F. Isin. Toronto: University of Toronto Press, 2008. As quoted in Bendixsen, Synnove K.N., 'Becoming Members of the Community of Value: Ethiopian Irregular Migrants Enacting Citizenship in Norway', *Migration Matters,* edited by Mahni Dugan and Arnon Edelstein, 3–22. Oxford: Inter-Disciplinary Press, 2013.

Dugan, Mahni and Arnon Edelstein. *Migration Matters*. Oxford: Inter-Disciplinary Press, 2013.

Edelstein, Arnon, 'Intimate Partner Femicide (IPF) Among Ethiopian Women in Israel'. *Migration Matters*, 141–166. Oxford: Inter-Disciplinary Press, 2013.

Grieco, Elizabeth M. et al. 'The Size, Place of Birth, and Geographic Distribution of the Foreign-Born Population in the United States: 1960 to 2010'. *Population Division Working Paper* 96, 3. Washington, D.C.: U.S. Census Bureau, 2012.

Halvorsrud, Kristoffer, 'Negotiating the Economic Duties of Citizenship: White South Africans in the UK and Belonging through 'Hard Work'', *Negotiating Boundaries in Multicultural Societies*, 3–32. https:///www.gv.com/lib/unconcious-bias-at-work. Viewed 15 July 2015. http://unctad.org/Sections/wcmu/docs/c1em30p004_en.pdf Viewed 19 July 2018.

Levrau, Francis, 'Esteem and Respect in a Multicultural Society: A critical Analysis of Axel Hometh's Recognition Theory', *Migration Matters,* 167–190.

Luong, Francis, 'Separating Illiberal from Liberal People', *Negotiating Boundaries in Multicultural Societies*, 81–100.

Mansour, Dina and Andrew Milne, *Negotiating Boundaries in Multicultural Societies*. Oxford: Inter-Disciplinary Press, 2014.

Sandel, Michael J., *Democracy's Discontent: America in Search of a Public Philosophy*. Cambridge: The Belknap Press of Harvard University Press, 1996.

Smith, Susan J., 'Comment: Citizenship: All or Nothing?', *Political Geography* 14:2 (1995): 190–193.

UN-DESA and OECD, 'World Migration in Figures (2013)'. Paper presented to the United Nations High-Level Dialogue on Migration and Development. http://www.oecd.org/els/mig/World-Migration-in-Figures.pdf.

PART 2

Citizenship and the State

Minimum Income Standard as a Social Citizenship Benchmark

The Case of Portugal

Maria Inês Amaro and Francisco Branco

Abstract

This chapter proposes to revisit the T.H. Marshall theory of citizenship stressing its present relevance. Departing from the author's concept of social citizenship, an analysis of the relevance of defining a decent standard of living for social policy is developed. Particularly, it is argued that the adoption of a minimum protection policy or a normative and civilizational reference safeguarding fundamental rights of citizenship in Portugal is required. We intend to highlight the consistency between Marshall's conception of social citizenship, anchored in the right to a modicum standard of economic welfare and security, and the theories of human needs. In addition, we discuss the consistency between his vision of right to civilizational inheritance attained in one's own community and consensual approaches, which favours a historical and cultural context of patterns of need satisfaction, transparency, democratic and public discussion and social construction of thresholds of human dignity safeguards. Based at theoretical, methodological and empirical levels, on the research project Minimum Income Standard in Portugal, undertaken since January 2012 by researchers from Lisbon University and Catholic University of Portugal, this chapter consists of an exploratory analysis of the citizen's rationalities when discussing what one should have to attain an adequate standard of living in Portugal. Data was collected qualitatively by means of nine focus groups, corresponding to the initial stage of the field work of the research project (orientation groups). Findings point to the existence of sensitive contact points, summed up as the reference to the five giants of social policy; the concern with safety and security, and the reference to prevailing standards.

Keywords

T.H. Marshall – social citizenship – decent standard of living – human needs – consensual approach – Portugal

© KONINKLIJKE BRILL NV, LEIDEN, 2022 | DOI:10.1163/9789004429253_004

1 Social Citizenship, Human Needs and the Definition of a Minimum Standard of Living

T.H. Marshall in his essay 'Citizenship and Social Class' conceptualises citizenship as consisting of three distinct elements which emerged in the last three centuries: civil rights, political rights and social rights.[1]

Civil rights emerged in the 18th century as an institutional protection of individual freedoms and equality before the law. This included the right to property and contract, the right to freedom of thought, expression and religious beliefs, the right of association, the right to economic initiative, and so forth.

Political rights, established in the 19th century, referred to the right to participate in the exercise of political power and, in particular, the right to elect and be elected and the right to take part in public governance and institutions.

Social rights, institutionalised in the course of the 20th century, relate to social services and benefits translating into the guarantee of a minimum standard of living according to given historical circumstances. These rights are, in Marshall's perspective, endeavoured mainly through social services and the education system.[2]

Despite the influential role of this approach till today, some limits to this theory have been pointed out. The most relevant critique to this conceptual framework addresses the question of Marshall's evolutionary vision of citizenship, with social rights being the corollary of its full attainment or realization. Some will argue that there is no basis to claim that social rights constitute the final stage of citizenship. On the one hand, with social welfare systems established, the so-called developed societies witnessed the emergence of new generations of rights; and, on the other, the most recent political and economic events gave ground to austerity policies which retracted social rights, challenging what Roche called the dominant paradigm of social citizenship.[3]

In fact, Marshall underlined the tension between capitalism and social citizenship, expressed in the unequivocal argument: 'citizenship and the capitalist class system have been at war'.[4] In this context the perspective of citizenship, as a problem of inclusion and exclusion, following Marshall's thought, gained a new centrality.[5]

1 T.H. Marshall, *Citizenship and Social Class* (London: Pluto Press, 1992 [1950]).

2 Marshall, *Citizenship and Social Class*, 8.

3 Maurice Roche, *Rethinking Citizenship* (Cambridge: Polity Press, 1992), has already pointed out issues of cultural citizenship, non-racial and non-sexist citizenship, ecological citizenship, global citizenship, and so forth.

4 Marshall, *Citizenship and Social Class*, 18.

5 Bart van Steenbergen, ed., *The Condition of Citizenship* (London: Sage, 1994), 1–9.

But without devaluing the relevance of this debate, we mainly emphasize what seems to be a critical contribution of his thought: his idea of social citizenship.

> By the social element I mean the whole range from the right to a modicum of economic welfare and security to the right to share to the full in the social heritage and to live the life of a civilised being according to the standards prevailing in the society.[6]

In line with this vision, Harris later points out that

> Social policies should be directed toward guaranteeing a range of life chances to the citizens of society. The relevant life chances are those required to protect the status of individuals as full members of the community. Their purpose is to offer material opportunities to participate in the way of life of the society [...]. An individual is «in need» for the purpose of social policy to the extent that he lacks the resources to participate as a full member of society in its way of life.[7]

Marshall emphasizes the importance of a basic provision of universal nature as a means of creating a platform of greater social equality based on social solidarity.[8] This issue, which re-emerged both during the 1990s debate on social policies and the crisis of the welfare state and today, as we witness the shrinkage of the welfare system, was clearly anticipated by Marshall.

As Bobbio points out, human rights, as fundamental as they are, are historical rights, born in certain circumstances, characterized by struggles in defence of new freedoms against old powers, and born gradually, not all at once, or once and for all.[9]

A link might be established between Marshall's conception of social citizenship and the theories of human needs, namely the works of Doyle and Gough on human needs theory and Nussbaum's version of capabilities approach.[10]

---

6 Marshall, *Citizenship and Social Class*, 8.

7 Len Doyal and Ian Gough, *A Theory of Human Need* (London: Palgrave Macmillan, 1991), 51.

8 Nancy Frase and Linda Gordan, 'Civil Citizenship against Social Citizenship', *The Condition of Citizenship*, ed. Bart van Steenbergen (London: Sage, 1994), 98–107.

9 Norberto Bobbio, *A Era dos Direitos* (São Paulo: Editora Campus, 1992), 5–6.

10 Ian Gough, 'Lists and Thresholds: Comparing the Doyal-Gough Theory of Human Need with Nussbaum's Capabilities Approach', *Capabilities, Gender, Equality: Towards Fundamental Entitlements*, ed. Flavio Comim and Martha Nussbaum (Cambridge: Cambridge University Press, 2014), 357–381; Martha Nussbaum, *Women and Development – The Capabilities Approach* (Cambridge: Cambridge University Press, 2000).

The first is centred on the definition of eleven intermediate needs and the other identifies ten central capabilities.[11]

2 The Consensual Approach to Determine an Adequate Standard of Living in Contemporary Societies

Marshall's vision of right to civilizational inheritance attained in one's own community might be grasped by consensual approaches, which favour the exploration of people's social construction of thresholds of human dignity. This is in line with the methodological framework of the research on Minimum Income Standard in Portugal (RAP), developed since January 2012 and from which data was extracted for this chapter. Let us present a brief overview of the project and its methodological bases.[12]

In scientific terms, RAP's main proposal is to reintroduce the estimation of income adequacy in the Portuguese poverty research agenda, focusing on the idea that minimum standards depend on the social, cultural and historical contexts and entails a social choice that requires public discussion and democratic understanding and acceptance.[13]

The project applied the budget consensual approach that replicates, with adequate adaptation, the design of the Minimum Income Standard for Britain.[14] In sum, the methodological design implied a refusal of a normative or expert-based approach and privileged the hearing of people for the construction of concrete budgets for everyday life, following an emergent trend

11 The eleven intermediate needs are: adequate nutritional food and water, adequate protective housing, a non-hazardous work environment, a non-hazardous physical environment, appropriate health care, security in childhood, significant primary relationships, physical security, economic security, safe birth and childbearing and basic education; The ten capabilities are: life, bodily health, bodily integrity, senses, imagination and thought, emotions, practical reason, affiliation, other species, play and control over one's environment.

12 José António Pereirinha, coordinator; Elvira Pereira; Francisco Branco; Maria Inês Amaro; Dália Costa; and Francisco Nunes, 'Project Rendimento Adequado em Portugal', reference: PTDC/CS-SOC/123093/2010 developed in partnership by University of Lisbon and Catholic University of Portugal: viewed 30 June 2015, www.fct.pt, see also www.rendimentoadequado.org.pt.

13 As in Amartya Sen, *Development as Freedom* (New York: Oxford University Press, 1999), 78–79.

14 Johnathan Bradshaw, et al., *A Minimum Income Standard for Britain: What People Think* (York: Joseph Rowntree Foundation, 2008) and Noel Smith, et al., *A Minimum Income Standard for Northern Ireland* (York: Joseph Rowntree Foundation, 2009).

in European and Anglophone research.[15] In his revision of more recent works on standard budgets, Fisher argues for the advantages of budget standard approach:

> not only the experts but also members of the general public can clearly see the style of life that families on the budget would be leading [...] in contrast, it is much more difficult to discern clearly what style of life is implied by a poverty line set at a particular percentage of median income, or a poverty line calculated using a particular multiplier and food plan.[16]

Walker, one of the foremost authors in the introduction of the consensual budget approach, stressed the deep limitations of survey techniques to produce a social consensus about basic or essential needs.[17] He uses the term, coined by Mack and Lansley, 'consensus by coincidence' to capture the nature of the consensus produced in surveys by contrast with 'consensus by consent' or compromise presented in interactive processes of consensus potentiated by group discussions.[18] This second approach is particularly sensitive when we are aiming at establishing a poverty threshold that ought to be related with the societal origin of the criteria by which any level of living is judged to be a reasonable minimum.[19]

This is the methodological orientation adopted by the Portuguese project, which combines consensual budget standards, based on focus groups with

---

15 Bradshaw, et al., *A Minimum Income Standard for Britain*; Gordon Fisher, *An Overview of Recent Work on Standard Budgets in the United States and Other Anglophone Countries* (2007), viewed 30 June 2015, http://aspe.hhs.gov/poverty/papers/std-budgets/report.pdf; Stella Hoff, et al., *The Minimum Agreed upon. Consensual Budget Standards for the Netherlands* (The Hague: The Netherlands Institute for Social Research, 2010); Bérénice Storms and Karel Van den Bosch, *What Income Do Families Need for Social Participation at the Minimum? A Budget Standard for Flanders* (2009), viewed 30 June 2015, https://www.cnle.gouv.fr/IMG/pdf/Synthese_etude_CSB-octobre2009_Beatrice_STORMS.pdf; Christopher Deeming, 'Minimum Income Standards: How Might Budget Standards Be Set for the UK?', *Journal of Social Policy* 34.04 (2005): 619–636.

16 Fisher, *An Overview of Recent Work on Standard Budgets in the United States and Other Anglophone Countries*: 4.

17 Robert Walker, 'Consensual Approaches to the Definition of Poverty: Towards an Alternative Methodology', *Journal of Social Policy* 16.02 (1987): 213–226.

18 Joanna Mack and Stewart Lansley, 'How Poor Is too Poor? Defining Poverty', *Poor Britain*, ed. Joanna Mack and Stewart Lansley (London: George Allen and Unwin, 1985), 15–48.

19 John Veit-Wilson, *Setting Adequacy Standards: How Governments Define Minimum Incomes* (Bristol: Policy Press, 1998), 11.

average citizens,[20] with expert budget standards approach, to estimate an adequate level of income for social functioning.

3 Citizen's Rationalities When Discussing What One Should Have to Reach an Adequate Standard of Living: The Case of Portugal

Based on a series of nine focus groups involving 68 people, it was possible to achieve some results concerning what people think would be an adequate standard of living.[21] These groups were held in three different regions of Portugal, which combined north/south and urban/rural characteristics, and were divided into three different types: 3 groups of people above 65 years old, groups of active age adults without kids in the household, 3 groups of active age adults with kids in the household.

The composition of each group was thoroughly prepared to ensure a balance in terms of features like gender, age, education level and socio-economic level. Hence, the general idea was to explore the views of the typical Portuguese on what an adequate standard of living might be. The group discussions took place in October 2012.

Following, we relate the obtained results with Marshall's views on citizenship and on what a modicum standard would be.

A *Minimum Needs, Dignity and Survival*

When we look at people's perspectives on minimum needs, we understand how influential Beveridge's vision of the Big Five of social policy was. Indeed, Health, Housing, Education, Social Protection and Employment cover most of the discussions endeavoured in the focus groups.[22] This is also not far from Doyal and Gough's considerations on a human's intermediate needs.

---

20 Meaning as close as possible to the 'typical' Portuguese.

21 This corresponds to the first phase of data collection of the project Adequate Income for Portugal – the Orientation Groups, which main objective was to discuss ideas of adequate living and reach a consensual definition of minimum standard of living (go to www.rendimentoadequado.org.pt to learn more about the project),viewed 25 January 2016, http://www.rendimentoadequado.org.pt/images/rap/pdfs/Boletim_RAP_1red.pdf.

22 William Beveridge authored, in 1942, the *Report on Social Insurance and Allied Services* which was highly influential for the foundation of social welfare systems and for the acknowledgment of five main areas of social security: health, employment, education, housing and social protection. Those became known as the five giants of social security, referential for the analysis of welfare systems.

It was common to all groups that the idea of the minimum must contain health, food, housing, sanitation and electricity, means of mobility (whether by car or public transportation), culture, sport and leisure and work.

Concerning this last, it was considered that employment is one of the most important needs that ought to be achieved as a minimum, as it is the basis of everything else and is the main source of personal development and self-fulfilment. As one participant argues, 'The access to work, which is the big and serious problem today, that makes that we don't get other minimums [...]'[23]

In fact, work was put in the centre of the minimum for an adequate standard of living, following a view that it is through work, and the income it provides, that people have access to all other critical 'must-have areas' for an adequate lifestyle.

It also strongly emphasized the references to stability and security as important for a minimum standard. These references implied two different meanings: a basic and an ontological one. As for the first, the issue of security was related with the protection from criminality and the presence of the police. For the second, it concerns the inner feeling of certainty and protection. Let us look at what participants actually stated, '[...] a stable source of income which keeps the person out of the degradation of mental health [...]'[24]

Discussions about minimums indicate that people put the standard above the survival line. In fact, participants shared their views about the way they think the concept of a life with dignity relates with survival possibilities. In a way, the concept of dignity was used as a term of differentiation of our humanity as opposed to our animalism. One participant referred, 'we are more than just the animals that need to survive, that need a shelter ... we are more than that'.[25]

In this sense, during the group discussions participants associated the idea of dignity with such things as caring about others (older people), being able to participate in social life (active adults with no kids) or not having the permanent feeling of being in-need, which means staying beyond the survival line. It is, as a matter of fact, an understanding of dignity as something which elevates human beings to a higher level of maintenance, which is however the minimum for them as humans.

Following this rationality, participants were prompt to argue that, in spite of being above survival; the standard of dignity is well below luxury and the sphere of desire. At this point, the discussions came close to a translation into

23 Female2_FocusGroup3_VNG_pp.123–124.

24 F2_FG2_VNG_p.510.

25 F4_FG3_VNG_pp.112–113.

practical guidelines of what Marshall's modicum would imply. Just to highlight a few arguments,

> Just to subsist is not enough to live with dignity; one has to have something else, enough to spend in culture, in health and to invest in one's well-being, which includes, once in a while, having some time to relax.[26]

But also, 'To live with dignity is not to have everything'.[27]

As we can see, references to dignity also overcome the mere material sphere and point out to the individual's feeling of being capable of responding to their own and to their loved ones' own needs and aspirations. It was in that sense that some groups associated dignity with the fact of having a job, not just because of the income, but also because of the sense of usefulness and capability it brings with it.

> Dignity would be having access to school, to decent housing, to a reasonable income, without luxurious thoughts, but that could give room to feed some dream of something, even to foresee children's education [...][28]

B *Citizenship and Well-Being*

Citizenship and well-being seem to be an overarching theme when discussion proceeds around what should be an adequate standard of living to live with dignity. Having a decent life implies, according to our discussion groups, being recognized as citizen, with overall duties and rights. That is, if the statute of citizenship is not granted, the standard of living would be below dignity. Moreover, it was mentioned that being a citizen implies a system, a structure, and a frame of services provided and/or assured by the state. '[...] ultimately, it is the state that has to provide, towards which I claim the rights [...]'[29]

This recalls Marshall's idea that the establishment of a minimum implies a position on the extent of inequalities considered legitimate and a role for the state in granting that that legitimacy is not broken.[30]

In some ways, all groups referred that living a decent life implies a certain level of freedom, whether it has to do with being able to make choices, with

26 Male10_FG1_VFX_p.66.

27 F3_FG2_VNG_p.115.

28 F5_FG2_BEJ_p.70.

29 F1_FG2_VFX_p.26.

30 Marshall, *Citizenship and Social Class*, 33.

stability and security, with access to the structures of rights' promotion or, most importantly, with having the opportunity to change the initial social position, to moving forward. In sum,

> [...] that I have the possibility of grabbing the tools to get out from the position I'm in. Let me use a picture: I'm in the quicksand, I have to think that I can't move a lot, 'cause if I do, I'll drown, I have to grab on to the good tools to get me out of the quicksand [...]'.[31]

Well-being will, then, be understood as a sum of material, physical, psychical, spiritual, moral and social satisfaction, where the social structure plays a central role.

Additionally, more abstract characters were highlighted by active adult groups as critical aspects for well-being. These concern things like trust, hope, security and safety and draw our attention back to Marshall's definition of social citizenship, when he argues that it is about the right to a modicum of economic welfare and security. Indeed, 'Security, security ... for a person to live, (he) must have security ...'[32]

The whole idea is that one should be released from fear and from barriers to self-fulfilment to be considered a full-rights citizen and to achieve well-being and these, not related with desire or luxury, will establish a minimum line for adequate living.

C *Putting Minimums in Context: The Adequate Standard for Today's Society*

Marshall's definition of social citizenship also refers to the right to share to the fullest in social heritage and to live according to the standards of prevailing society.[33] It is interesting to analyse how the focus groups referred to the minimum in relation to present Portuguese society.

Generally, groups acknowledged that dignity, when applied to the assessment of standards of living cannot be understood without a social, cultural and historical context. A life with dignity is always seen in relation to the society in which it evolves and to the historical time of reference. Hence, there were references to both the importance of comparability and to the importance of cultural patterns in use. Participants referred to this in the following

31 F1_FG2_VFX_p.200.

32 M6_FG3_VFX_p.27–28.

33 Marshall, *Citizenship and Social Class.*

terms, '[…] each community has its own basics, not all communities have the same necessities […]'.[34]

Most participants seem to understand this relation between minimums and civilizational patterns as entailing a tendency of growth. That is, the overall perspective is developmental, meaning that as time passes the pattern of minimum ascends to new, more demanding, thresholds. Following that line of thought, we would say that today's societies have higher minimums than societies in the past and that what was luxurious fifty years ago is a basic need at present. In this sense, thinking of dignity as more than just surviving results from a civilizational breakthrough.

The main aspects put forward as a result of the relation of minimums with today's society were the ones related to mobility and communication, both arising from technological advances.

As far as mobility is concerned, the need to have a car was advocated by many participants. The possession of this asset, however, was not consensual among all groups as it was more substantiated among the ones who have kids and the ones who live outside cities, where the public transportation network is not so reliable. 'Nowadays, the car is not a luxury, (it) is a need'.[35]

Communication and information technologies were abundantly referred to as paramount in present societies. The arguing rational for that varied from justifications based on what others have that one should have too for the sake of social integration; to the need to access services, job' opportunities; security; sociability, and so forth. Hence, assets like TV sets, mobile phones, computers or internet connections were generally accepted as part of what everyone should have. The following statements gave ground to the understanding of information and communication technologies as part of basic needs:

> […]Today, the entire world has access to mobile communication, it is not considered a luxury at all … to have a computer, to have an internet connection, it is the essential basics.[36]

It was quite clear that there is an immediate relationship established between what is considered to be a minimum and the kind of society we are referring to, mostly in respect to information and communication technologies' use. If we could refer to present society as a technological one, we might see here how

34 M3_FG2_VFX_p.133.
35 M1_FG2_VNG_p.404.
36 F6_FG3_VFX_pp.370–371.

people engage with the social heritage of their own society and plan to take their share.

4 Concluding Remarks

As an exploratory exercise, it was possible to signal consistencies between Marshall's view on social citizenship and what a number of today's typical Portuguese citizens referred to when asked to discuss minimums to achieve an adequate pattern of life with dignity.

The most sensitive contact points were:

- The reference to the five giants of social policy;
- The concern with safety and security, and
- The reference to the prevailing standards.

Another significant aspect to consider is the definition of acceptable minimum living standard in Portugal as participants conceived it:

A decent (or acceptable) minimum standard of living nowadays in Portugal, includes, in addition to food, housing and clothing, all that is needed for a person to be healthy, feel secure, to relate to others and feel respected and socially integrated. This includes free and informed choices about practical things of life and forms of personal fulfilment, as access to education and work, culture and leisure.[37]

If we consider this definition, it is possible to establish a sound relationship of this acceptable minimum standard, not only with Marshall's vision of social citizenship, but also with its firm anchorage in the human needs/central capabilities conceptions of Doyle and Gough and Nussbaum, respectively, with regards to basic human needs, such as health and security, social integration and participation.

Bibliography

Bobbio, Norberto. *A Era dos Direitos* [*The Age of Rights*]. São Paulo: Editora Campus, 1992.

Bradshaw, Johnathan, Sue Middleton, Abigail Davis, Nina Oldfield, Noel Smith, Linda Cusworth, and Julie Williams. *A Minimum Income Standard for Britain: What People Think*. York: Joseph Rowntree Foundation, 2008.

37 raP, *Boletim RAP #1* (2013): 3, viewed 25 January 2016, http://www.rendimentoadequado.org.pt/images/rap/pdfs/Boletim_RAP_1red.pdf.

Deeming, Christopher. 'Minimum Income Standards: How Might Budget Standards Be Set for the UK?'. *Journal of Social Policy* 34.04 (2005): 619–636.

Doyal, Len and Ian Gough. *A Theory of Human Need.* London: Palgrave Macmillan, 1991.

Fisher, Gordon. *An Overview of Recent Work on Standard Budgets in the United States and Other Anglophone Countries.* 2007. Viewed 30 June 2015, http://aspe.hhs.gov/poverty/papers/std-budgets/report.pdf.

Frase, Nancy, and Linda Gordan. 'Civil Citizenship against Social Citizenship'. *The Condition of Citizenship,* edited by Bart van Steenbergen, 98–107. London: Sage, 1994.

Gough, Ian. 'Lists and Thresholds: Comparing the Doyal-Gough Theory of Human Need with Nussbaum's Capabilities Approach'. *Capabilities, Gender, Equality: Towards Fundamental Entitlements,* edited by Flavio Comim and Martha Nussbaum, 357–381. Cambridge: Cambridge University Press, 2014.

Hoff, Stella, Corinne van Gaalen, Arjan Soede, Albert Luten, Cok Vrooman and Sanne Lamers. *The Minimum Agreed upon. Consensual Budget Standards for the Netherlands.* The Hague: The Netherlands Institute for Social Research, 2010.

Mack, Joanna and Stewart Lansley. 'How Poor Is Too Poor? Defining Poverty', edited by Joanna Mack and Stewart Lansley, 15–48. London: George Allen and Unwin, 1985.

Marshall, T.H. *Citizenship and Social Class.* London: Pluto Press, 1992 [1950].

Nussbaum, Martha. *Women and Development – The Capabilities Approach.* Cambridge: Cambridge University Press, 2000.

Nussbaum, Martha. 'Capabilities as Fundamental Entitlements: Sen and Social Justice'. *Feminist Economics* 9.2–3 (2003): 33–59.

raP, *Boletim RAP #1.* 2013. Viewed 25 January 2016, http://www.rendimentoadequado.org.pt/images/rap/pdfs/Boletim_RAP_1red.pdf.

Roche, Maurice. *Rethinking Citizenship.* Cambridge: Polity Press, 1992.

Sen, Amartya. *Development as Freedom.* New York: Oxford University Press, 1999.

Smith, Noel, Viet-Hai Phung, Abigail Davis and Donald Hirsch. *A Minimum Income Standard for Northern Ireland.* York: Joseph Rowntree Foundation, 2009.

Steenbergen, Bart van, ed. *The Condition of Citizenship.* London: Sage, 1994.

Storms, Berenice and Karel Van der Bosch. *What Income Do Families Need for Social Participation at the Minimum? A Budget Standard for Flanders.* 2009. Viewed 30 June 2015. https://www.cnle.gouv.fr/IMG/pdf/Synthese_etude_CSB-octobre2009_Beatrice_STORMS.pdf.

Veit-Wilson, John. *Setting Adequacy Standards: How Governments Define Minimum Incomes.* Bristol: Policy Press, 1998.

Walker, Robert. 'Consensual Approaches to the Definition of Poverty: Towards an Alternative Methodology'. *Journal of Social Policy* 16.02 (1987): 213–226.

Citizenship as an Egg?

Y.Y. Brandon Chen

Abstract

Pursuant to the 'liberal nationalist' account, citizenship is simultaneously exclusive and inclusive. Its particularistic aspect functions as a fence that keeps non-members out while its universalistic element acts as the glue that binds all members. In theory, any tension between these seemingly competing attributes is reconcilable as they are assigned to distinct spatial domains, the former to citizenship's exterior and the latter interior. Thus, often drawing comparison to an egg, citizenship is said to consist of a hard shell and a soft centre. In this chapter, I rely on a historical review of international migrants' shifting healthcare entitlement in Canada as a lens for contesting this liberal nationalist portrayal of citizenship. I observe that, on its edges, the exclusionary propensity of Canadian citizenship is sometimes reined in by inclusionary norms to enable the entry of even migrants commonly characterised as undesirable because of their suspected dependence on public healthcare. Conversely, in Canadian citizenship's interior, complete realisation of universal healthcare has been thwarted by particularistic welfare controls that query foreign residents' labour market contributions and the genuineness of their humanitarian needs. As such, contrary to the proverbial egg, citizenship is actually not as hard on the outside or as soft on the inside.

Keywords

Canada – citizenship – international migrant – healthcare – human rights

1 Introduction

Citizenship, according to the Supreme Court of Canada, represents 'membership in a state', and 'in the citizen inhere those rights and duties, the correlatives of allegiance and protection, which are basic to that status'.[1] It denotes a legal institution that both anchors and delimits a sociopolitical space in which members of a sovereign nation supposedly exercise civic rights and

1 *Winner v. S.M.T. (Eastern) Ltd.* [1951] S.C.R. 887, 918.

© KONINKLIJKE BRILL NV, LEIDEN, 2022 | DOI:10.1163/9789004429253_005

responsibilities on an equal basis. In other words, citizenship is simultaneously exclusive and inclusive. It functions as a fence that keeps non-members out as well as the glue that binds all members together with a promise of universalism. In theory, any tension between citizenship's particularistic and universalistic attributes is reconciled as these seemingly contradictory logics are assigned to distinct domains of citizenship, the former to its exterior while the latter interior. Thus, often drawing comparison to an egg, this 'liberal nationalist' account of citizenship is said to consist of hard edges and a soft center.[2] As the metaphor goes, the borders of nation-states resemble the shell of the citizenship egg and secure the warm and fuzzy ideals of egalitarianism solely for those located within state territories qua members.

In reality, however, the correspondence among various facets of citizenship such as territorial presence, membership status and rights is much messier than what the liberal nationalist conception suggests. In a world of porous borders, not only is complete spatial segregation of members and non-members virtually untenable, it is also not uncommon for foreign nationals who are de jure non-members in host countries to be afforded rights similar to citizens. Conversely, the discourse of 'second-class citizens' illustrates the possibility for individuals with formal membership status to nevertheless be denied rights and protections that are part and parcel of citizenship's substance due to discrimination.[3] As such, rather than engaging in a precise division of labour, citizenship's particularistic and universalistic impulses are more accurately understood as being locked in a tug of war both on its geographic edges and in its interior. At the border, citizenship's exclusionary propensity is reined in by inclusionary norms, which in turn enables the admission of some individuals despite their designation as non-members. Likewise, inside citizenship's physical space, complete realization of universalistic aspirations is frequently thwarted by particularistic forces that continue to exert their influences beyond the border. Contrary to the proverbial egg, citizenship is arguably not as hard on the outside or as soft on the inside. Absence of official membership standing does not necessarily preclude one from entering citizenship's spatial domain; at the same time, territorial presence is no guarantee of being granted membership rights, either. If we are to redeploy the egg analogy, substantive membership in a state — in terms of full enjoyment of civil, political

2 Linda Bosniak, 'Ethical Territoriality and the Rights of Immigrants', *Amsterdam Law Forum* 1.1 (2008): 4.

3 Linda Bosniak, 'Constitutional Citizenship through the Prism of Alienage', *Ohio State Law Journal* 63.5 (2002): 1313.

and social rights as articulated by T. H. Marshall[4] — is better conceived of as the yolk, with access thereto doubly guarded by a semi-permeable shell and the viscous white.

In this chapter, I set out to examine the evolution of international migrants' healthcare entitlement in Canada through the prism of such a modified account of citizenship. In so doing, I hope to examine how citizenship's external and internal particularistic machineries interwork to regulate healthcare entitlement as a civic right. I contend that international migrants' ability to secure public healthcare coverage is indicative of their possession of the social dimension of substantive citizenship. The attainment of such citizenship rights, namely the yolk of the citizenship egg, is in turn dictated by the interplay between what has been termed 'immigration control' (i.e. the shell) and 'welfare control' (i.e. the egg white).[5]

2 Immigration Control and Migrant Healthcare Entitlement

Canadian immigration law has long prohibited the border entry of international migrants who are perceived as burdens on public coffers due to their health conditions. Up until the late 1970s, the admission of international migrants found living with disabilities or contagious diseases, and sometimes even that of their accompanying family members, were generally forbidden.[6] Following the passage of the *Immigration Act, 1976–77*, Canada replaced such a blanket ban with a more discretionary approach that barred the border entry of only those who were considered a likely threat to public health or public safety, and those who might reasonably be expected to impose excessive demand on health and social care.[7] However, the absence of precise governmental guidelines on what constituted 'excessive demand' made immigration officials' decision-making highly subjective, and as a result left many seemingly legitimate migrants still inadmissible. Today, the 'excessive demand' prohibition persists under the *Immigration and Refugee Protection Act*, although

4 T. H. Marshall, 'Citizenship and Social Class', *Citizenship and Social Class and Other Essays*, ed. T. H. Marshall (London: Cambridge University Press, 1950), 10–11.

5 Ed Mynott, Beth Humphries and Steven Cohen, 'Introduction: Locating the Debate', *From Immigration Controls to Welfare Controls*, eds. Steven Cohen, Beth Humphries and Ed Mynott (New York: Routledge, 2002), 1–2.

6 *Immigration Act*, S.C. 1910, c.27; *An Act to Amend the Immigration Act*, S.C. 1919, c.25; *Immigration Act*, S.C. 1952, c.42.

7 *Immigration Act*, S.C. 1976–77, c.52.

an exemption from inadmissibility has been created for refugees as well as foreign spouses and children of Canadians that are being sponsored to come to Canada as family-class immigrants.[8] Arguably, for individuals deemed medically inadmissible, immigration policies rather than Medicare eligibility rules pose the foremost barrier to their healthcare entitlement in Canada.

Occasionally, Canadian courts have allowed otherwise inadmissible migrants to enter the country by requiring them to trade off their rights to social and healthcare benefits.[9] The Canadian federal government's push in the past decade to admit elderly family-class migrants through a special visa program that affords no healthcare entitlement represents a similar trade-off between border entry and rights to health and social support.[10] In both instances, medical inadmissibility policy is substituted by cost-shifting measures that privatise government's healthcare obligations. Therefore, in what appears to be government giving with one hand and taking away with the other, international migrants who have traditionally been characterised as undesirable have been conditionally allowed to penetrate Canada's borders.

The influence of immigration controls on migrant healthcare entitlement extends beyond the very moment of border entry determination, however. According to the *Canada Health Act*, Canada's public healthcare insurance, known as Medicare, must be made available to all eligible 'residents' defined as persons who are 'lawfully' entitled to be or to remain in Canada.[11] As such, for migrants who enter through unsanctioned pathways or who fall out of status while in the country, immigration controls continue to haunt them inside Canada's territorial boundaries and impede these migrants' access to Medicare.

3 Welfare Control and Migrant Healthcare Entitlement

Although cooperative schemes designed to facilitate healthcare access for an entire community had been springing up in rural Canada since the early 1900s, Canadian Medicare did not come into existence until after the Second World War. Introduced in 1957 as a national hospital insurance program, Medicare

8 *Immigration and Refugee Protection Act*, S.C. 2001, c.27.

9 *Hilewitz v. Canada (Minister of Citizenship and Immigration)* [2005] 2 S.C.R. 706; *Companioni v Canada (Minister of Citizenship and Immigration)*, 2009 FC 1315.

10 Canada, Citizenship and Immigration Canada, 'Government of Canada to Cut Backlog and Wait Times for Family Reunification – Phase I of Action Plan for Faster Family Reunification' (News Release, Ottawa, 4 November 2011).

11 *Canada Health Act*, R.S.C. 1985, c.C-6.

was expanded a decade later to include coverage for necessary care provided by medical practitioners.[12]

The establishment of Medicare was underpinned by a universalistic aspiration. According to then Health Minister, A. J. MacEachen, the advent of Medicare rested on the 'fundamental principle that health is not a privilege tied to the state of one's bank account, but rather a basic right which should be open to all'.[13] As such, in its early decades, Medicare coverage was relatively accessible to everyone in Canada regardless of citizenship and immigration status. For international migrants, once they managed to get past border control and related hurdles, their access to public healthcare was greatly facilitated by Medicare's universalistic tenor.

It was not until circa 1985 that the provinces started to scrutinise prospective Medicare applicants' eligibility more closely, and in the process, international migrants' healthcare entitlement became gradually scaled back. Over the years, the availability of public healthcare to international migrants in Canada has become more contingent on the administrative statuses that migrants are assigned at border entry, their labour market engagement and, for humanitarian migrants, the perceived authenticity of their claims. In other words, whereas during the first decades of Medicare, immigration controls acted as the primary barrier to migrants' access to the Canadian healthcare system, today this fence is buttressed by healthcare eligibility rules that separate migrants into those who are deemed self-sufficient, desirable and deserving and those who are characterised as high users of public resources, fraudsters and undeserving.

In this section, I will illustrate international migrants' decreasing healthcare entitlement in Canada by examining two specific instances of legislative change: Ontario's Medicare reform in the early 1990s, and the nationwide expulsion of asylum seekers from Medicare that began in 1986 and culminated in the introduction of the Interim Federal Health Program a decade later.

3.1 *Ontario's Medicare Reform*

Before the mid-1990s, eligibility rules for the Ontario Health Insurance Plan (OHIP) were relatively lenient. Pursuant to the province's *Health Insurance Act* in effect at the time, OHIP coverage was prima facie available to all residents irrespective of their citizenship and immigration statuses provided that they

12 Malcolm Taylor, *Health Insurance and Canadian Public Policy: The Seven Decisions That Created the Canadian Health Insurance System and Their Outcomes* (Kingston: McGill-Queen's University Press, 2009), 234, 374–375.

13 Canada, *House of Commons Debates*, 12 July 1966 (A. J. MacEachen), 7545.

had up-to-date authorization to stay in Canada, were ordinarily present in Ontario and were not tourists, transients or visitors.[14] To satisfy the ordinary presence requirement, OHIP beneficiaries only needed to spend at least four consecutive months in Ontario every year so long as they made the province their permanent home. Once qualified residents registered for OHIP, they were immediately issued a unique health number, which they and their dependents could use to access publicly financed healthcare services without having to undergo any waiting period.

Beginning in the late 1980s, there were growing concerns in Ontario that the provincial government's chronic under-enforcement of the OHIP eligibility rules was allowing some people that lacked legal entitlement to nevertheless secure healthcare coverage. News media regularly featured stories about suspected misuses of OHIP by ineligible people, including: Quebec residents who hoped to receive services not covered at home by obtaining OHIP coverage using their Ontario work addresses; expatriates who retained their health numbers and used them to acquire out-of-country treatment; uninsured U.S. citizens who sought free care in Canada with OHIP numbers that they purchased on the black market; and foreign visitors who borrowed the health numbers of their Canadian relatives to receive emergency care.[15]

Further fuelling the public's worries about OHIP fraud, an internal government study conducted in 1993 estimated that fraudulent claims were costing Ontario's healthcare system $284 million a year.[16] However, the study problematically conflated two distinct issues under the rubric of fraud. On the one hand, it raised the alarm about individuals without legal entitlement being able to secure OHIP coverage through illegitimate means. On the other hand, it took aim at certain foreign residents that were legally entitled to OHIP benefits for their supposedly questionable health-seeking behaviours. Painting both issues with the same brush represented a discursive sleight of hand where foreign residents and legitimate OHIP beneficiaries became the new focal point of a struggling government campaign to curb unauthorised healthcare access. In other words, what started out as a criticism of the Ontario government's poor management of its healthcare registration system was transformed into a condemnation of international migrants' purported abuse of their OHIP

14 *Health Insurance Act*, R.S.O. 1990 c.H-6.

15 Chris Hall, 'Bill for Ottawa OHIP Faker: $30,000', *Ottawa Citizen*, 14 March 1990, B1; Derek Ferguson, 'OHIP Cheats Got Posh Cures at U.S. Clinics', *Toronto Star*, 15 March 1990, A12; Maria Bohuslawsky, 'Hospitals Helpless against OHIP Fraud Artists', *Ottawa Citizen*, 20 March 1990, B2.

16 Kevin Donovan, 'Health Card Abuse Called "Rat's Nest"', *Windsor Star*, 18 August 1993, A1.

coverage. This discursive shift, facilitated by the sweeping language of fraud, saw international migrants increasingly portrayed in the popular media not as legitimate OHIP beneficiaries but as health tourists who reportedly moved to Canada only to receive free healthcare or to give birth to their children who would be granted Canadian citizenship.[17]

In 1994, amidst an escalating debt load and recurring budget deficits, public concerns about Medicare fraud in Ontario came to a head and caused the government to introduce a series of restrictions on who could qualify for OHIP. Reflecting the prevailing narrative, a good number of these new measures targeted international migrants specifically. Both foreign students and asylum seekers were expressly excluded from OHIP. While the government initially also eliminated the OHIP coverage of all temporary foreign workers and their dependents, it later reinstated the benefits of migrant workers and their families if they had proven plans to stay in the province for at least three years.[18] According to government officials, the policy reversal was motivated by a desire to encourage migrants with steady jobs to settle in Ontario on a long-term basis. To the extent that this policy objective accorded with Canadian immigration law's valorization of migrants who were perceived as more capable of self-sufficiency, it signalled a growing convergence between immigration and welfare controls in the country.

Other elements of Ontario's Medicare reform in 1994, while facially neutral, also affected international migrants' OHIP eligibility disproportionately. For example, the government decided to impose a three-month wait on all new OHIP applicants.[19] Such waiting periods tended to impede the healthcare access of newcomers to Canada particularly because, unlike people moving to Ontario from another province, they lacked an existing public healthcare insurance plan to fall back on. Similarly, migrants also bore the brunt of the adverse consequences of the government's move toward an individualised OHIP eligibility assessment model. In an effort to combat fraudulent use of OHIP cards by ineligible persons, the government introduced a brand new health card with strengthened security features and required each Ontario resident to obtain the card by way of re-registering for OHIP.[20] Whereas in the past, dependents of an OHIP beneficiary could qualify and register for the

17 Matt Maychak, 'Foreigners Exploit Health Cards: MPP', *Toronto Star*, 22 October 1992, A17; Ellen van Wageningen, 'Fighting Fraud: The Ontario Health Ministry Is Seeking Ways to Police Health-Card Abuse', *Windsor Star*, 21 August 1993, F1.

18 Caroline Mallan, 'Province Reverses Another OHIP Cut', *Toronto Star*, 23 July 1994, A11.

19 Elizabeth Payne, 'Ontario Tightens OHIP Rules', *Ottawa Citizen*, 2 April 1994, A1.

20 Lisa Priest, 'Photo OHIP Cards Meant to Combat Fraud', *Ottawa Citizen*, 4 May 1994, A3.

programme automatically, they must now establish eligibility in their own right. This meant that some migrants in mixed-status families, such as foreign spouses of Canadians who were in the country on visitor visas while awaiting the results of their permanent residency applications, were no longer entitled to OHIP.

3.2 *Asylum Seekers' Exclusion from Medicare*

Asylum seekers' successive removal from provincial Medicare programs across Canada between circa 1985 and circa 1995 represented another instance of migrant healthcare retrenchment in Canada in recent decades. Like the OHIP reform in the early 1990s, this policy development was aided by both an increasingly popular narrative that portrayed asylum seekers as abusers of the healthcare system, and a concomitant rise in the Canadian society's comfort level in relying on Medicare eligibility rules as reinforcement of its immigration control agenda.

Up until the mid-1980s, asylum seekers in all provinces except Alberta received public healthcare insurance through Medicare. In 1986, British Columbia became the first among the Canadian provinces that previously provided Medicare coverage to asylum seekers to reverse their policies. As justification, the Health Minister of British Columbia at the time argued that it was 'improper for Canada to permit a person into the country who then require[d] extensive medical care and then to say to the provinces: "Pick up the tab"'.[21] As such, the provincial government's message was clear. Asylum seekers were depicted as visitors who were in Canada mainly for the pursuit of free healthcare, and insofar as the immigration system had failed to weed out these health tourists, it was the federal government that must assume the financial consequences.

British Columbia's decision to eliminate asylum seekers' Medicare coverage triggered a domino effect across the country. By the time that Ontario moved to eliminate asylum seekers' OHIP coverage in 1994, Quebec was the only province left that still granted Medicare entitlement to this population. That too was discontinued in 1996.[22] Throughout this process, the imagery of asylum seekers qua health tourists continued to be invoked by the provinces as a cause for concern. Besides the discourse in Ontario mentioned above, Quebec's move to strip off asylum seekers of their Medicare entitlement was in part dressed up by the government as a last resort to correct an unfair financial

21 Canada, British Columbia, Legislative Assembly, *Hansard*, 10 April 1986 (Jim Nielsen), 7679.

22 Philip Authier and Samana Siddiqui, 'Refugee Claimants to Lose Health Benefits', *Gazette* (Montreal, QC), 15 June 1996, A1.

burden of having to provide for asylum seekers who came from countries that supposedly did not produce genuine refugees.[23] To the extent that the spectre of fraudulent asylum seekers also prompted the federal government to tighten the country's refugee rules around the same time,[24] the changes in asylum seekers' Medicare eligibility brought the logic of Canada's welfare controls ever closer in line with that of its immigration regulations.

In response, the federal government began assuming the healthcare expenses of asylum seekers in 1994. Initially, healthcare providers were reimbursed by Health Canada for services rendered, but since April 1995, asylum seekers' healthcare has been financed through the Interim Federal Health Program (IFHP) administered by Citizenship and Immigration Canada.[25] The move to transfer the asylum seeker healthcare program to the federal immigration portfolio made explicit the ongoing encroachment on the Canadian refugee healthcare policies by border management-related calculus. To this day, immigration control remains a central consideration in Canada's decision-making concerning asylum seekers' healthcare entitlement. As a case in point, between June 2012 and April 2016, the federal government extensively pared down the scope of the IFHP such that the extent of asylum seekers' healthcare coverage became generally correlated with the perceived authenticity of their asylum claims.[26]

4 Conclusion

The concept of citizenship commonly evokes both particularistic and universalistic aspirations. It looks to demarcate a political community by singling out non-members for exclusion as well as to nurture a shared identity and a sense of belonging among members. Some legal and political theorists have sought to resolve the tension between these seemingly conflicting features of citizenship by assigning them to different spatial domains: exclusionary forces to the borders and inclusionary ideals to within the political community. Accordingly, citizenship is said to have an egg-like property: hard on the outside and soft on

---

23 Ibid.

24 Mary Williams Walsh, 'A Lamp to the Nations Flickers', *Los Angeles Times*, 18 June 1992, 1.

25 Canada, Citizenship and Immigration Canada, *Operational Manual: Reference, IR 3, Medical* (Ottawa, 2010), 4–5.

26 Canada, Citizenship and Immigration Canada, 'Reform of the Interim Federal Health Program Ensures Fairness, Protects Public Health and Safety' (News Release, Ottawa, 25 April 2012).

the inside. In this chapter, I challenge the validity of this account of citizenship in a world where international migration is a reality. On the one hand, the continued presence of international migrants in Canada suggests that the egg shell of citizenship is more porous than the liberal nationalist notion of citizenship contends. On the other hand, the upswing of welfare controls in recent decades and their alignment with the established immigration-control agenda show that the centre of citizenship as an egg is not always marked by egalitarian ideals. Thus, for international migrants, citizenship's substance, including the right to healthcare, is restricted by mechanisms that operate both at the exterior and the interior of a political community. If citizenship as a bundle of rights is at all like an egg, it is better conceived of as the egg yolk. Access thereto requires international migrants to penetrate both a semi-permeable shell in the form of border controls and the gooey egg white that represents an increasing array of welfare restrictions that are being implemented across receiving countries.

Bibliography

An Act to Amend the Immigration Act, S.C. 1919, c.25.

Authier, Philip and Samana Siddiqui. 'Refugee Claimants to Lose Health Benefits'. *Gazette* (Montreal, QC), 15 June 1996.

Bohuslawsky, Maria. 'Hospitals Helpless against OHIP Fraud Artists'. *Ottawa Citizen*, 20 March 1990.

Bosniak, Linda. 'Constitutional Citizenship through the Prism of Alienage'. *Ohio State Law Journal* 63.5 (2002): 1285–1325.

Bosniak, Linda. 'Ethical Territoriality and the Rights of Immigrants'. *Amsterdam Law Forum* 1.1 (2008): 1–9.

Canada. *House of Commons Debates*, 12 July 1966.

Canada. British Columbia, Legislative Assembly. *Hansard*, 10 April 1986.

Canada. Citizenship and Immigration Canada. 'Government of Canada to Cut Backlog and Wait Times for Family Reunification – Phase I of Action Plan for Faster Family Reunification'. News Release, Ottawa, 4 November 2011.

Canada. Citizenship and Immigration Canada. *Operational Manual: Reference, IR 3, Medical* (Ottawa, 2010).

Canada. Citizenship and Immigration Canada. 'Reform of the Interim Federal Health Program Ensures Fairness, Protects Public Health and Safety'. News Release, Ottawa, 25 April 2012.

Canada Health Act, R.S.C. 1985, c.C-6.

Companioni v Canada (Minister of Citizenship and Immigration), 2009 FC 1315.

Donovan, Kevin. 'Health Card Abuse Called "Rat's Nest"'. *Windsor Star*, 18 August 1993.

Ferguson, Derek. 'OHIP Cheats Got Posh Cures at U.S. Clinics'. *Toronto Star*, 15 March 1990.

Hall, Chris. 'Bill for Ottawa OHIP Faker: $30,000'. *Ottawa Citizen*, 14 March 1990.

Health Insurance Act, R.S.O. 1990 c.H-6.

Hilewitz v. Canada (Minister of Citizenship and Immigration) [2005] 2 S.C.R. 706.

Immigration Act, S.C. 1910, c.27.

Immigration Act, S.C. 1952, c.42.

Immigration Act, S.C. 1976–77, c.52.

Immigration and Refugee Protection Act, S.C. 2001, c.27.

Mallan, Caroline. 'Province Reverses Another OHIP Cut'. *Toronto Star*, 23 July 1994.

Marshall, T. H. 'Citizenship and Social Class'. *Citizenship and Social Class and Other Essays*, edited by T. H. Marshall, 1–85. London: Cambridge University Press, 1950.

Maychak, Matt. 'Foreigners Exploit Health Cards: MPP'. *Toronto Star*, 22 October 1992.

Mynott, Ed, Beth Humphries and Steven Cohen. 'Introduction: Locating the Debate'. *From Immigration Controls to Welfare Controls*, edited by Steven Cohen, Beth Humphries and Ed Mynott, 1–8. New York: Routledge, 2002.

Payne, Elizabeth. 'Ontario Tightens OHIP Rules'. *Ottawa Citizen*, 2 April 1994.

Priest, Lisa. 'Photo OHIP Cards Meant to Combat Fraud'. *Ottawa Citizen*, 4 May 1994.

Taylor, Malcolm. *Health Insurance and Canadian Public Policy: The Seven Decisions That Created the Canadian Health Insurance System and Their Outcomes*. Kingston: McGill-Queen's University Press, 2009.

Van Wageningen, Ellen. 'Fighting Fraud: The Ontario Health Ministry Is Seeking Ways to Police Health-Card Abuse'. *Windsor Star*, 21 August 1993.

Williams Walsh, Mary. 'A Lamp to the Nations Flickers'. *Los Angeles Times*, 18 June 1992.

Winner v. S.M.T. (Eastern) Ltd. [1951] S.C.R. 887.

I Am the Three Percent

Amanda Bigler

Abstract

This chapter is a creative nonfictional account of being detained and subsequently deported at Heathrow Airport in May of 2013. The piece explores the stringent and contradictory practices of the United Kingdom Border Agency (UKBA). The overzealous and harassing nature of the UKBA has been detailed in several comparative articles, and there are instances where people who should not have been were detained. Overall, the piece works to show a first-hand account of the UKBA detention, its centres, and its practices.

Keywords

UKBA – detention – Serco – deportation – visa – Heathrow

1 Border Control[1]

Browsing through the daily news at my desk in my student flat, a headline caught my eye: 'Journalist's partner interrogated at Heathrow for nine hours'.[2] I would not consider myself the most philanthropic sort of person, nor am I one who is necessarily intrigued by the hardships of journalists with regards to foreign policy. The words, rather, captivated me for personal reasons.

'Only nine hours?' I spat, spinning my chair around with raised eyebrows. 'Big deal. Try eleven capped off by another thirteen in a detention centre.'

---

1 Editors' note: Every effort was made to contact the author to gain her permission for the publication of this chapter. Unfortunately, we were unable to. However, given that the author has made an initial submission for publication, we have taken the liberty to include her work here.

2 Mark Duell, 'Edward Snowden Journalist Glenn Greenwald's Partner David Miranda Detained at Heathrow Airport', *Daily Mail*, August 2013, Viewed on 18 August 2013, http://www.dailymail.co.uk/news/article-2396745/Edward-Snowden-journalist Glenn-Greenwalds-partner-David-Miranda-detained-Heathrow-airport.html.

© KONINKLIJKE BRILL NV, LEIDEN, 2022 | DOI:10.1163/9789004429253_006

These episodes happen to international travellers, no matter their affiliation. I packed my messenger bag and headed out in the English breeze towards the university campus, thoughts swirling around my head like bothersome banshees. The past two months had been a whirlwind of emotional chaos, none of them, apparently, newsworthy.

Home is a trickily defined word. After only eight months in England, I had begun to call the small East Midland town my own. I had thrown away vocabulary such as 'trash can' and 'block' and replaced them with 'bin' and 'you know, right down the street'. I embraced the country that had given me the opportunity to advance my studies, to create a life away from the sepia lens of Kansas. Each time a clerk in Topeka or Kansas City would ask me for my identification on my holiday, I would proudly show them my passport.

'Yes,' I would say, with a smug smile, 'I'm living in England now. I'm moving into a new flat in September.'

What is the classification for someone who no longer feels as if she belongs to her mother country, but does not have the rights of the new country either? The term 'ex-patriot' comes to mind, but the negative connotation surrounding it does not describe the feeling of confusion and displacement I felt when asked to describe my nationality. In England, I would sheepishly reply, 'American, but I'm not conservative and I hate guns!' In America, I would say, 'Oh, yeah, I just guess I fit in better across the pond. You know, better opportunities. Less student debt'.

On the plane ride from Charlotte, North Carolina to London, England, I watched the monitor in front of me, mapping out the distance in both kilometres and miles from North Carolina to home. The small, animated plane slid slowly across the mapped Atlantic, and I became too excited to sleep. It had been a week and a half since I had left the East Midlands, and I was ready to return to life. Each flickering move of the 3D plane propelled me closer to the country I had adopted.

I pulled the twenty kilos of luggage I had been able to check on the plane through the corridors and over the several hundred meter entrance to the opening of the United Kingdom Border Agency (UKBA) room. I was standing in the immigration queue patiently.

'Next please!' a voice shouted.

I bustled up to the counter and gave the officer my documents, anticipation overcoming my fatigue and lack of nourishment.

'How long where you in the UK in January?' The man asked, his thin face and freckled nose glaring down at me.

'In January? Three weeks.' I replied. I was disconcerted by the judgmental look in his eyes, but tried to stave off the emotion.

'Do you have a return ticket?'

'Not yet. I'm planning on booking it next month,' I said, smiling as I held out my hand to retrieve my passport. He stared at my open palm, then gestured at the chairs on the right of the desk.

'We have an issue. Have a seat over there, please.'

His voice was authoritative and low and I felt my heart slide down into my shoe. I was going to miss my train, and I felt naked without my passport in hand. Peering across the barrier, I watched as three workers in uniform talked in a huddle, shiftily looking at me. I regretted packing the peanut butter in my suitcase. A year earlier, the airport security had thought the peanut butter in my mother's luggage was a bomb.

2 Detention Questioning

'Come with me.' a woman with a thick Indian accent said sharply, her heels clipping against the hard floor as I rushed to follow her with my enormous suitcases.

The room I was placed in consisted of a row of chairs, a small television mounted on the wall, a vending machine, and a payphone. I had been in the waiting area of an American jail once, and the sentiment of the room was eerily similar. The fluorescent lights beamed down on my head, and I began to sweat. The woman left me at the front of the room and gestured to a man in the locked surveillance window.

'Heya, I just need to take your items for inventory.' he said to me.

His smile was genuine, though it gave little comfort to me. My hands were shaking so forcibly that I could not wheel my suitcases into the small, glass room.

'Stand right there, yeah? Just not inside here.'

I watched as he opened each bag, my purse, and my laptop case. After searching through my underwear, the damned jar of peanut butter, and a large, blown-up portrait of my sister's face on a stick, he refastened the zipper. He tied off the bags with neon-coloured plastic locks, and ushered me to one of the chairs.

'Can I call someone?' I asked. *Would a lawyer be too cliché for an American?* I thought.

'Sure, if you have a UK number,' he answered.

The only number I knew, the only one I wanted to call, was my partner. I was not allowed to touch my cell phone, but after giving the worker my pass code, he retrieved the number I needed. When I finished briefing my partner of the situation, I buzzed the guard once more.

He had been looking through the photos on my phone, and my neck bristled at the invasion.

'Why don't you, ah, look at those papers there,' the worker said, hurriedly turning off my cell phone guiltily. 'They'll explain a bit.'

I sat down and began to read:

> NOTICE TO DETAINEE, REASONS FOR DETENTION AND BAIL RIGHTS:
> c: Your removal from the United Kingdom is imminent.
> 7: You have not produced satisfactory evidence of your identity, nationality or lawful basis to be in the UK.[3]

My palms grew clammy, sticking to the pages. A flush of cold rushed through my veins, and I began to panic. I dropped the document on the chair and pressed the buzzer.

'Yes?' The man asked.

'I ... I ... I don't know ... don't understand ... wha-what's happening,'

The tears came swift and strong, and my nose began to clog with snot. The man looked at me with pity, ushered me back to the chair, and explained that I needed to wait to talk to someone.

'Can I ... I ... I have a cigarette?'

'There's no smoking here.' he replied.

'I ... I underst-stand. Can I ... have ... my notebook?'

He retrieved my spiral from my purse, and I felt calmed by having the familiar pencil in my hand. I began to write. I wrote for hours, jotting down descriptions of the room, the worry my parents and my partner must be experiencing, and thoughts as profound as 'I don't understand why I'm here'. Around 13:00, my name was called.

'Amanda ... Big-ler?' The voice asked, the same Indian accent that had given me the UK Border Agency document.

'Yes?' I asked blearily, closing my notebook and standing to meet her.

'Come in here.'

I followed her into the room. She closed the door behind us, and I sat in the hard, plastic chair. I forced my eyes not to tear up yet again, and instead

3 Home Office, 'Notice to Detainee: Reasons for Detention and Bail Rights', (UKBA, 19 May 2013), 1.

focused on the papers in front of me. After stating that I did, in fact, speak English and did understand the allegation, the interrogation commenced.

'You said you were here for three weeks, but you were here for four months. Lying to an immigration officer could be punishable by a sentence or by deportation'.

Her look was cool and piercing, and she rattled her rings against the countertop as she waited for my reply. *Clink. Clink. Clink. Clack clack ... clink.*

'I didn't lie.' I said bluntly.

'You said you were here for three weeks,' she repeated.

'No, I said I was here for three weeks *in January*, as he asked. I thought, since he said January, he was going to go through each month'.

She scribbled furiously on the notepad in front of her.

'I believe you lied, and I believe you knew that you were lying,'

'No,' I said, my voice rising and cracking, 'He asked how long I had been here in January. I said three weeks. That wasn't a lie.'

'You don't have a return ticket?'

'No, not yet. The prices are supposed to go down, but we're in an airport. I can buy one right now if I'm allowed to.'

'No, once you've been detained, you can only have what you have.'

'It seems a bit silly. I can buy one right now. Problem solved.'

'No.'

When questioned about my intentions in the UK, I explained that I was a student and asked her to refer to the documentation I had given the man at the main desk.

'So what are you planning on doing after your studies?' She asked, rifling through the papers I had printed off before leaving the States.

'I'm planning on applying to a PhD program in either the UK or the Netherlands, or maybe France. My partner's from there, so I'm looking at the options right now.'

'So no set plans?'

I balked.

'Yes, yes I have plans. I just told you.'

'So no set plans.'

By three o'clock I was back in the main holding room. As I had not eaten in over twelve hours, I forced myself to accept an egg sandwich from the desk man. It was around five o'clock in the evening when the managing immigration officer beckoned me into the interrogation room. It had been nine hours since I had arrived at Heathrow. My limbs ached from sitting in hard chairs and sleeping in random places for the past thirty-six hours. The woman smiled at me and helped me into my seat.

'Amanda Bigler.'

'Yes.'

'I've reviewed this, I've already signed off on it, so there really isn't anything more that we can do.'

'But I'm a student, and my temporary visa hasn't expired.'

'I see that, but you need 'leave to enter' clearance. What you'll need to do, since this has already gone through, is to go back to America and renew your visa. We are going to hold you until tomorrow, and then you will be sent back.'

'I think I'm going to be sick,' I said, small lights popping from the back of my eyes.

The sweat and the cold returned to my body, and I could vaguely hear the woman say, 'If you need to be sick, you can go to the toilet.'

I tried to stand up, but it only furthered the swashing of sandwich in my stomach and the perspiration between my knees.

'Trash can,' I said, opting for the American term. I was no more a Brit than I was a tree. The disillusionment I had been under spewed out from my lips, as did the egg salad sandwich.

3 Serco Detention Facility

At 7:12 p.m. I was taken in an armoured van to a detention facility. I was shown the facility's physician, who took my height and weight. After having my blood pressure, my lungs, and my heart rate checked, I was released to the front desk. I had considered this a soothing courtesy, but looking at opendemocracy.net's information on Serco (opendemocracy.net being a major site that collects information on immigration rights and government practices), the detention company employed by the UKBA, there were different means other than 'courtesy' for the medical examination. The article purports 'Last year, there were three deaths in detention. There were also four separate instances where High Court judges have found the treatment of three individuals to amount to a breach of Article 3 of the European Convention on Human Rights, which prohibits "inhuman or degrading treatment" '.[4] Once I was transferred into the care of Serco, the company had to give me medical attention to compensate for

4 Natasha Tsangarides, 'Pregnant, Detained, and Subjected to Force in the UK', *Open Democracy*, 2012, Viewed on 18 August 2013, http://www.opendemocracy.net/5050/natasha-tsangarides/pregnant-detained-and-subjected-to-force-in-uk.

their negative reputation. Although Serco may have had issues in the past, at least they had trained their staff to be both sympathetic and kind.

'It's alright if ya smoke up there, love,' the worker at the desk said. 'Heaven knows ya need it.'

I was led up to the dormitories, and was given a private room.

'You're lucky there aren't more here. I think we can give you one of your own,' the warden said.

I used the computer for twenty minutes, contacting my partner via e-mail and telling him to get hold of my family. All social media applications where blocked, and the room's lights were turned off. The warden paced back and forth, making sure the door to the computer room remained open. I logged off and retrieved my toothbrush from the tiny plastic container issued to me. After brushing my teeth in the dimly lit, damp shower room, I opened the door to the room ... my room. I lay down on the hard, Styrofoam mattress of the concrete cot, and my eyes dry-heaved tears.

Though the UKBA does not keep regular public statistics on women detained due to immigration, information shows a general consensus that around 7,000 women are held in detention every year.[5] The company working with the Border Agency, Serco lined the walls with slogans and tips for the detention centre dormitory. Though they were meant, I assume, to reassure the detainees, signs such as 'We care' and 'We respect you' seemed rather facetious when being stripped of either care or respect.

I spent the entire night staring at the wall, picking at a hangnail, and contemplating the outcome for the two other detained women on the floor. The next morning I was notified of my departure by a knock on my door. For the first time I was content that I was being sent back to the United States, out of the limbo of detention.

I was taken down the elevator to the main desk, where my luggage was wheeled out. My purse had been placed in a Ziploc bag, and the worker escorting me loaded my belongings into the armoured van.

'Here you go.' said a large, boisterous woman at the desk. 'If you can just sign this, saying you've been given this pound in compensation for your stay, you'll be done here.'

I laughed in spite of my glum spirit as the golden pound winked up annoyingly at me.

5 Tsangarides, 'Pregnant'.

4 Visa Renewal

The plane ride back to the United States was both welcomed and resented. On one hand, I had my freedom, the ability to lay my seat back and watch a B rated movie across the Atlantic while eating honey roasted peanuts. On the other hand, I was leaving my home. I had been an hour and a half train ride away from my life, my studies and my friends.

'Hey, you were on the flight on Friday.' said one of the stewardesses in a North Carolina twang. 'Had a short layover as well?'

'Yeah, you could say that,' I said, clicking my seat belt and opening the sheer plastic covering of the blue plane blanket.

I had not showered in three days, had not eaten anything that stayed put for two days, and had a face that resembled someone who had either been in a boxing ring and had lost, or someone who had been stung by bees.

'This is for you, I believe. Amanda Bigler?'

'Yeah,' I said, wondering if it were possible to be detained mid-flight.

He handed me my passport, around it a rubber band holding in place my continuing ticket from Charlotte to Kansas City.

'Thanks,' I croaked.

I would have to surrender my passport a week later through the United States Postal Office to have the new visa attached to its pages.

After a month and a half staying in the United States, a five hour trip to Oklahoma City to have my biometric information taken, a four hundred pound visa renewal application fee, and a summer of over 100 degree weather (over 40 for Brits) I finally had my passport back in hand and was ready, once again, to return to the United Kingdom. For the remaining time I spent in Kansas, I had neither passport nor driver's license, and took to carrying around my university ID and my birth certificate for identification purposes. Stripped of my identity, I waded alone, not identifying with either country. I had spent the Fourth of July in the capital city of Kansas, Topeka. The irony of wanting so desperately to return to the country my forefathers had fought diligently to break away from was not lost on me.

I returned to the United Kingdom after a small hassle at Heathrow once more. My passport had been red-flagged for further scrutiny before entry. After calling both my partner and threatening to call the US embassy, I was granted entry clearance. Reading the news report only two days after was disheartening. I choked down my disgust when phrases such as 'public confidence in security powers depends on [UKBA processing] being used proportionately within the law, and also on having independent checks and balances in place to prevent misuse'[6] and 'According to official figures, more than 97 per cent of examinations ... last less than an hour, and only one in 2,000 people detained is kept for more than six hours'[7] flashed across the screen. I was embarrassed by the inner workings of the UKBA and was sceptical of their findings; apparently I fell into the 3 percent and within the one in 2,000.

6 Duell, 'Edward Snowden'.

7 Ibid.

PART 3

Citizenship in Education

Representations of Young Citizens in Aotearoa New Zealand's Schooling Curriculum

Philippa Hunter

Abstract

Are young people compliant, standardised, or agentive citizens in the making? How do they, or how might they, represent the future-oriented multi-literate citizens envisaged in Aotearoa New Zealand's schooling curriculum? The author's experiences as a teacher educator, and her sustained involvement in national history and social sciences curriculum and assessment initiatives, inform her interest in the cultural politics of curriculum. From a critical pedagogy stance, the chapter examines ways in which New Zealand's curriculum policy shaping conceptualises young citizens across thirteen years of primary and secondary years of learning. Accordingly, the national curriculum is conceived as a culturally constructed and contested site of intentions, pedagogical approaches, and standardised outputs. Cross-disciplinary notions of citizenship are examined in the contexts of curriculum policy, and discursive production. Whilst national curriculum decision-making 'plays out' through dynamic processes and structures, the enacted curriculum continues to socialise teachers and young people within enduring master narratives. Assumptions of who counts, or who is visible as a citizen in a future-focused society are viewed as questionable, particularly when legacies of nostalgia and desire frame experience. How might curriculum spaces and possibilities rethink citizenship and future-oriented narratives of representation?

Keywords

citizenship – curriculum – policy – representation – discourse – cross-disciplinary

1 Introduction

The chapter focuses on the educational context of Aotearoa New Zealand's national schooling curriculum and its cross-disciplinary policy shaping of young citizens. A critical pedagogy stance informed by a duality of resistance and reflexivity examines the cultural politics of curriculum as an organising

© KONINKLIJKE BRILL NV, LEIDEN, 2022 | DOI:10.1163/9789004429253_007

force in citizenship education. A conceptualisation of 'literacies of power' disturbs and counters normalised beliefs.[1] The question of how a national curriculum envisions young citizens in the making is considered. The dynamic nature of competing curriculum discourses is introduced, and Aotearoa New Zealand's citizenship foundations briefly described. Notions of citizenship are examined. The national curriculum's rise of explicit citizenship ideals is examined together with citizenship education research findings and public representations of citizenship identity and belonging. Concluding reflections about future-oriented lifeworlds young citizens move across, call for a reshaping of citizenship thinking.

2 Aotearoa New Zealand's Schooling Curriculum

The *New Zealand Curriculum* policy [NZC] is a curriculum compromise, where a range of visions and ideologies about curriculum purpose, agency, and desired educational outcomes for young New Zealand citizens co-exist. Policy compromise is reflective of groups in society that the curriculum represents.[2] Curriculum theorists have challenged ways schooling curriculum embed 'questionable assumptions' and a lack of critique of reproduced and enduring values.[3] Elliot Eisner observed that curriculum ideologies influence learners' socialisation. Consequently, these are maintained when we become teachers. Eisner described this process as 'professional socialisation'. This continuing process involves a curriculum's claims to knowledge, cultural values, traditions, practices and teacher interpretation.

---

1 Notions of 'literacies of power' shape the author's critical pedagogy stance. Three theorists in particular influence this thinking: Henry A. Giroux. 'Disposable Futures: Dirty Democracy and the Politics of Disposability', *Education and Hope in Troubled Times: Visions of Change for Our Children's World,* ed. H. Svi Shapiro (New York: Routledge, 2009), 223–241; Patricia Hinchey, *Becoming a Critical Educator. Defining a Classroom Identity, Designing a Critical Pedagogy* (New York: Peter Lang, 2004); Joe, L. Kincheloe, 'Critical Pedagogy in the Twenty-First Century: Evolution for Survival', *Critical Pedagogy: Where Are We Now?* eds. Peter McLaren and Joe L. Kincheloe (New York: Peter Lang, 2007), 9–43.

2 Ministry of Education, New Zealand, *The New Zealand Curriculum: For English-Medium Teaching and Learning in Years 1–13* (Wellington: Learning Media, 2007).

3 Elliot W. Eisner, 'Questionable Assumptions about Schooling', *Phi Delta Kappan,* 84.9 (2003): 648–657; Dave F. Brown, 'It's the Curriculum, Stupid! There's Something Wrong with It', *Contemporary Readings in Curriculum,* ed. Barbara Slater Stern and Marcella L. Kysilka (London: Sage, 2008) 291–298.

3 Curriculum and Competing Discourses

The notion of *discourse* is conceived as language and the ways ideas, values, and experiences are communicated to make meaning. Curriculum discourses embed visions and ideologies as active processes. The NZC policy comprises a range of internal discourses as values, disciplinary voices, and principles that compete noisily with each other. The ideas and beliefs about knowledge, pedagogy and cultural ideas that teachers implement in their practice reproduce discourses. Teachers' preferred practices might be seen as desired ways of seeing and doing 'played out' as discursive production. The cultural theorist Joe Kincheloe articulated discursive practices as a 'set of tacit rules that regulate what can and cannot be said, who can speak with the blessing of authority, and who must listen …'.[4] Discourses compete in New Zealand's curriculum and assessment policies and the enacted curriculum. Identified as loose groupings: *scholar traditional, learner centred/experiential, social constructionist* and *social efficiency*,[5] these discourses jostle and compete through curriculum intent, implementation, and standardised outcome. Their identification enables a clearer understanding of the policy representation and shaping of young people as New Zealand citizens.

4 Aotearoa New Zealand's Citizen Rights by Historical Treaty

The 1840 Treaty of Waitangi enabled Britain to establish sovereignty over New Zealand, legalise British subjects, and secure the economic benefits of imperialism. Two language and values-based treaties, the Treaty of Waitangi and Te Tiriti o Waitangi illuminate culturally encoded interpretations of sovereignty, and the ways indigenous Māori were merged with British subjects by Treaty article. David Pearson comments:

> Compared with politico-legal agreements in other British settler states … the Treaty paved the way for a unique subject/citizenship regime for Māori as, on the one hand, legally recognised co-members in the state and, on the other, as 'intimate others' with a recognised position within visions of a yet-to-be-created 'nation'.[6]

4 Joe, L. Kincheloe, ed., *Classroom Teaching: An Introduction* (New York: Peter Lang, 2005), 13.

5 Michael Schiro, *Curriculum Theory: Conflicting Visions and Enduring Concerns* (London: Sage, 2008).

6 David Pearson, 'Citizenship, Identity and Belonging: Addressing the Mythologies of the Unitary Nation State in Aotearoa/New Zealand', *New Zealand Identities: Departures and*

For Māori, colonising processes brought marginalised political representation, land loss, social and economic neglect and indifference for Treaty rights. Māori have never ceased to resist or seek redress for breaches of the Tiriti o Waitangi – viewed as a sacred covenant with the Crown. The relationship between indigenous Māori and Pakeha settlers is a central feature of subjecthood and citizenship in Aotearoa New Zealand's history of colonisation and decolonisation. New Zealand's citizenship status was created in 1948 by the *British Nationality and New Zealand Citizenship Act* that was replaced by the *Citizenship Act* of 1977 then amended in 2005. Ongoing migration is a further feature of citizenship and identity shaping, of the 'governance of the settler state'[7] and of increasing cultural pluralism.

5 Citizenship Conceptions

Ideals and practices of citizenship generally involve political freedom and choice, forms of economic and social equality and experiences of identity and belonging. Citizenship confers status in terms of a person's legal rights, and responsibilities of participation as a member of the nation state. Democratic values, government by due political processes and human rights, shape public practice through legislation, customs and traditions. This assumes a body of common political knowledge.[8] Participatory citizenship involves taking opportunities that living in a democracy provide to enhance the quality of life experiences. This may manifest as community-mindedness, participation in local organisations, social action and/or global awareness.[9] Conceptions of 'multiple citizenship'[10] reflect identity in relation to a range of affiliations including national, cultural, religious, indigenous, ethnic and political. Globalising processes provoke reassessment of citizenship as an identity tied to the nation state.[11] James Banks interrogated liberal, assimilationist, and universal conceptions of citizenship in seeking cultural rights for citizens of diverse cultures,

---

Destinations, eds. James Liu, Tim McCreanor and Teresia Teaiwa (Wellington: Victoria University Press, 2005), 21–37, 25.

7 Pearson, 'Citizenship, Identity and Belonging', 27.

8 Kathleen Knight Abowitz and Jason Harnish, 'Contemporary Discourses of Citizenship', *Review of Educational Research* 75.2 (2006): 653–690.

9 Carol Mutch, 'Citizenship Education: Does It Have a Place in the Curriculum?' *Curriculum Matters* (2005): 49–69.

10 Will Kymlicka, *Multicultural Citizenship* (Oxford: Oxford University Press, 1995).

11 Louise Humpage, 'Talking about Citizenship in New Zealand', *Kotuitui, New Zealand Journal of Social Sciences* 3 (2008): 121–134.

ethnicities, and languages.[12] Feminist and indigenous scholars have challenged assumptions of citizenship as a unitary and inclusive source of identity and belonging.[13]

The Royal Society of New Zealand's census findings show that New Zealand is 'increasingly a country with multiple cultural identities and values'[14] and that one in four people living in New Zealand in 2013 were born in places elsewhere than New Zealand. The Report states:

> The most important example of 'diversity' may be in the range of ideas about what is represented and what is valued. A longstanding and deep-seated desire on behalf of the majority community to identify as New Zealanders with a single set of values and practices will be even less apt than in the past.[15]

By increasing cultural diversity, this challenges unitary citizenship ideals and politically-focused citizen envisioning. As a powerful cultural construct, citizenship is shaped by dominant groups' values-laden discourses about who might identify and belong as a New Zealander. The schooling curriculum is also shaped by these values and ideals.

6 Citizenship Orientations in the National Curriculum

New Zealand's curriculum has an explicit citizenship educational aim: 'A framework designed to ensure that all young New Zealanders are equipped with the knowledge, competencies, and values they will need to be successful citizens in the twenty-first century'.[16] The NZC *Values* are: *excellence; innovation,*

---

12 James A Banks, 'Teaching for Social Justice, Diversity, and Citizenship in a Global World', *The Educational Forum* 68 (2004): 296–305.

13 Ruth Lister, 'Citizenship: Towards a Feminist Synthesis', *Feminist Review* 57 (1997): 28–48; Anne-Shela Orloff, 'Gender and the Social Rights of Citizenship: The Comparative Analysis of Gender Relations and Welfare States', *American Sociological Review* 58.3 (1993): 303–328; Mason Durie, *Te Mana, Te Kawanatanga. The Politics of Maori Self-Determination* (Auckland: Oxford University Press, 1998).

14 Royal Society of New Zealand, *Our Futures, Te Pae Tāwhiti: The 2013 Census and New Zealand's Changing Population* (Wellington: Royal Society of New Zealand, 2014), 3, viewed 10 January 2015, www.royalsociety.org.nz/expert-advice/papers/yr2014/our-futures/.

15 Royal Society of New Zealand, *Our Futures*, 8.

16 Ministry of Education, New Zealand, *The New Zealand Curriculum*, 4.

inquiry, curiosity; diversity; equity; community and participation; ecological sustainability; integrity and respect. These values might be intended to shape and provide students with emotional and social capabilities that enable them to adapt to the challenges they will face.[17] On the other hand, *Values*-led citizenship education might be seen as redefining politics, and undermining students' right to decide their social and political value-system.[18] The *Values* element of the national curriculum policy states: 'community and participation for the common good is associated with values and notions such as peace, citizenship, and manaakitanga'.[19] The NZC *Future Focus* guidance presents citizenship as 'exploring what it means to be a citizen and to contribute to the development and well-being of society'.[20]

Neither civics nor citizenship are taught as subjects in the national curriculum. Rather, they are integrated into *Learning Areas*, with contextual emphasis provided within the social sciences. Civics and citizenship ideals are tacitly and explicitly embedded in NZC *Principles*, *Values*, *Key Competencies*, and *Learning Areas'* achievement objectives. In government produced social sciences resource materials, further conceptions of citizenship are communicated. For example, citizenship is defined as 'the relationship between a person and their community'[21]: 'Students need opportunities to think critically about the issues associated with globalisation and how it affects their participation in society and responsibilities towards others'[22]; 'The [resource book] will examine concepts related to behavioural economics, including needs, wants, the consumer, and the producer, and link these to the concept of citizenship'.[23]

The NZC learning areas' statements embed the policy's citizenship imperative and communicate desired citizenship outcomes. The NZC learning areas' statements of nature and purpose identify discursive orientations of

17 Leon Benade, 'Shaping the Responsible, Successful and Contributing Citizen of the Future: "Values" in the New Zealand Curriculum and Its Challenge to the Development of Ethical Teacher Responsibility', *Policy Futures in Education* 9.2 (2011): 151–162. doi: 10.2304/pfie.2011.9.2.151.

18 Kevin Rooney, 'Citizenship Education: Making Kids Conform', (2007), np, viewed 5 September 2014, http://www.spiked-online.com/index.php?/site/printable/4023/.

19 Ministry of Education, New Zealand, *The New Zealand Curriculum,* 10.

20 Ibid., 39.

21 Ministry of Education, New Zealand, *Belonging and Participating in Society: Building Conceptual Understandings in the Social Sciences* (Wellington: Ministry of Education, 2008), 5.

22 Ministry of Education, New Zealand, The Publication of *Being Part of Global Communities* BCUSS Series 15 (Wellington: Ministry of Education, 2011), 2.

23 Ministry of Education, New Zealand, The Publication of *Financial Literacy*: BCUSS Series 15 (Wellington: Ministry of Education, 2011), 4.

citizenship ideals as: *Contributory or active participation, informed or discerning, responsibility, identity,* and *critical.* The active participation focus reflects strong learner-centred experiential discourse in conceptions of social sciences and technology curricula. The social sciences' Social Inquiry methodology supports participatory action through its emphases on inquiry, values, perspectives thinking, and social decision-making. Technology signals participatory action through creative and innovative problem solving. English, the arts, health and physical education, and science statements reflect contributory citizenship discourses involving dispositions and skills of wellbeing, interaction, innovation, and guardianship of finite resources. Informed and discerning citizens are envisaged in half of the learning areas including the arts learning area that seeks citizens who can communicate and lead enriching lives. The responsible citizen is represented across the social sciences, languages, and health and physical education learning areas. Qualities of responsible citizens include cultural understandings, social responsibility, and social justice. Identity discourses are evident in the social sciences in relation to values clarification, as consumer identities in technology, as personal in the arts, and through notions of national identities in languages. Critically engaged citizens are envisaged as reflective decision-makers in the social sciences, socially just citizens in health and physical education and citizen-science guardians in the field of science. Ideas of critical citizens align with social reconstructionist curriculum discourse in seeking 'better social worlds' and 'improving' societal issues in the present.

7 Rise of Explicit Citizenship Ideals in Curriculum

Teachers in the social sciences/studies community have long understood citizenship discourses in relation to a continuum indicating transmissive pedagogy – or critical pedagogies of counter-socialisation.[24] Prior to the NZC implementation, citizenship across the curriculum was relatively benign.

24 Hugh Barr, John Graham, Philippa Hunter, Paul Keown and Judith McGee, *A Position Paper: Social Studies in the New Zealand School Curriculum,* Ministry of Education, New Zealand: Social, Physical and Health Education Department, School of Education (Hamilton, University of Waikato, 1997); Diana Hess, 'Controversial Issues and Democratic Discourse', *Handbook of Research in Social Studies Education,* eds. Linda Levstik and Cynthia Tyson (New York: Routledge, 2008), 124–136; Anna Ochoa-Becker, 'Socialization and Counter Socialization for a Democracy', *Democratic Education for Social Studies: An Issues-Centred Decision Making Curriculum* (New York: Information Age Publishing, 2007), 65–100.

The social sciences assumed responsibility for inquiry-based learning around civics-based studies of formal institutions and processes. The interdisciplinary social studies included socio-cultural, historical, geographic and economic understandings to support political themes and contexts. The 2007 *NZC* policy shift emphasized issues of rights, roles, and responsibilities in secondary social studies, as a means to encourage citizenship-focused study. However, contexts tend to reflect dominant narratives, and teachers' custom and practice preferences. Teachers are under increasing pressure to produce desired outcomes and normative subjects/citizens who are economically productive, socially responsible, and responsive to government policies. Explicit cross-curricula citizenship intentions and outcomes for students' learning and assessment are a recent phenomenon. In the senior secondary years, the *NZC* aligns with standards-based assessment that embeds social efficiency/managerial discourse. Drawing on social studies for example, curriculum and assessment alignments have resulted in achievement standards, whereby senior students are examined by standards that present social action as good works and altruism in contexts of participatory citizenship.

8 Wider Curriculum Citizenship Representations

A proliferation of curriculum initiatives in response to wider social concerns is apparent in New Zealand schools. The Ministry of Education has developed learning stories, and school case studies to exemplify these initiatives. *Citizenship* has become a key theme for school programmes, and for reporting successful student engagement. In curriculum and school stories, citizenship is invoked to represent positive expressions and actions of school identity, unity of purpose, and pride. Interestingly, a strong civics and citizenship orientation underpins the development of programmes such as education for sustainability, traffic and road safety, blood services, taxation education, school gardens, healthy eating, safe sex, and financial literacy. Students are represented in these programmes as good citizens who are taking responsibility for their futures. Likewise, the values and competencies of digital citizenship and cybersafety directly reference the curriculum, and a 'digital citizen' is described as understanding the rights and responsibilities of inhabiting cyberspace.[25]

---

25 Ministry of Education, New Zealand, *Teaching Digital Citizenship* (Wellington: Ministry of Education nd.), viewed 1 June 2015, http://elearning.tki.org.nz/Teaching/Digital-citizenship#definition.

9 Citizenship Education Research

New Zealand was a participant country in the 2008 *International Civic and Citizenship Education Study* [ICSS].[26] Of 38 participating countries, 21 had civics and citizenship taught as subjects. In New Zealand these were contextually integrated within the social studies curriculum. The New Zealand research participants comprised 3,900 Year 9 students aged 13–14, 1400 teachers, and 120 principals. New Zealand students' mean scores of civic knowledge were above the ICCS average. However, whilst a number of students had a very sound civic knowledge, many had poor civic knowledge. The gap was wider than any other participating ICCS country. This appears to indicate civic disengagement and social exclusion of young citizens whereby civic knowledge is connected with socio-economic circumstances. The ICCS methodology conceptualised three types of citizens:

i. The personally responsible citizen who pays tax, obeys the law, recycles, volunteers;
ii. The participatory citizen who is active in community organisations, makes efforts to care for those in need, cleans up the environment;
iii. The justice-oriented citizen who critically assesses social, political, and economic structures to see beyond surface causes.

Students' responses represented the personally responsible citizenship orientation. However, principals and teachers viewed students' critical and independent thinking as a key aim of citizenship education, and the school experience as enabling forms of student representation in civic activities.

A recent research study 'Citizenship and Participation of Young People in Aotearoa/NZ'[27] shows young people define citizenship in relational, inclusive and diverse terms. Their thoughts about citizenship are expansive, and go beyond future-orientated neoliberal discourses that position them in terms of economic independence and employment. Young people experience social membership predominantly through leisure, sport, cultural and non-structured activities, rather than through traditional civic and political associations. They place importance on a sense of belonging. They are interested and

26 New Zealand Government, *ICSS: International Civic and Citizenship Education Study*, Managed by the Ministry of Education, under the auspices of the International Association for the Evaluation of Educational Achievement [IEA] (Wellington: New Zealand Government, 2008–2012), viewed 1 November 2012, https://www.educationcounts.govt.nz/publications/series/iccs.

27 Philippa Wood, 'Citizenship and Participation of Young People in Aotearoa/New Zealand' (MA Thesis, Massey University, 2013).

engaged in both informal and organised activities that enable them to relate to other young people. How does this relational citizenship orientation sit with public discourses of identity and belonging?

10 Citizenship Representation and Public Discourse

Dominant citizenship visions are evident in national identity narratives that emphasise Aotearoa/New Zealand's sporting achievements at home, and globally. As a small Pacific nation of 4.6 million people in 2016, enduring narratives of nationhood ideals represent New Zealand as 'punching above its weight' and as a force for competition and achievement in many fields such as science, sport, innovation, cultural relations. A legacy of desire and nostalgia frames these narratives of lived experience. In 2015, the cricket world cup was played in New Zealand and Australia. This event generated nostalgia in the media about the 'gentleman's game', and families playing backyard cricket in sunny quarter acre sections and on beaches. The media reported the competition as unifying the country in terms of national pride and excitement. National identity forged by lives lost in overseas theatres of war is another enduring narrative of sacrifice and nationhood that shapes citizenship discourses. Commemoration of the centenary of New Zealand's participation in the World War 1 Gallipoli campaign (1915), with its massive loss of lives, has dominated a collective consciousness. Significant government funding of national and community activities has included educational involvement, through cross-curricula resourcing of WW1 contexts for inquiry across primary and secondary years of learning.

Comfortable identity narratives are currently disrupted by media representations of ISIL, movements of boat people from Indonesian waters, Treaty of Waitangi settlements, Maori sovereignty, social disparities of wealth and home ownership, the user pays economy and downsized public services, educational commodification, discourses of standards, teacher de-professionalism and under achievement. Consequently, who is visible as a citizen today, and who counts into the future? Images that represent New Zealand people and society are powerful. Influential New Zealanders on prime time television regularly voice identity claims such as: 'But you're still an immigrant, not a real New Zealander!'; 'You haven't been here long enough to call yourself a New Zealander'; 'Kiwis can always be seen by their 'can do' approach'. A prevailing public discourse of strongly held beliefs that we're good at human rights has been challenged by recent research that shows New Zealand is slipping in its adherence to 6 major human rights treaties, since its signings in the 1970s.[28] Critical issues of child poverty, gender equality, systemic disadvantage of Maori and rights of disabled people that challenge the state call into question the relationship between human rights and citizenship.

11 Possibilities and Closing Thoughts

Should the schooling curriculum shape standardised compliant citizens within policies of longing that aim to preserve political and social institutions, and processes? Or, should the curriculum envision and shape multi-literate agentive citizens to participate within and across rapidly changing lifeworlds? The idea of citizenship within lifeworld challenges mainstream discourses of citizens living in a common world with homogenised and disembodied citizenship or 'citizenship without lifeworld'.[29] Hung reminds us that the view of the citizen as representative of a community overlooks the citizen's 'individual idiosyncrasies and uniqueness – the lifeworld'.[30] Hung visualises a civic community as an open domain that welcomes diversity. We need to understand students' lifeworlds, respond to their questions, and promote open dialogue. Students in the senior years of the school history curriculum have expressed their preferences for learning contexts that focus on the antecedents of sexism, racism, and issues that play out globally in the twenty-first century.[31] Significantly, it is through social media that young people feel a sense of belonging, make a stand, or collectively respond to social issues and causes that resonate with their lifeworlds, and identity work. For example, in 2014, New Zealand secondary students used social media to organise rallies to protest the Nigerian Boko Haram's kidnapping of schoolgirls. Likewise, students across 40 schools formed anti-bullying campaigns, and joined in mute protest to draw attention to the harassment of gay students.

The experiences and perspectives new teachers and students bring to curriculum and pedagogy could well be shared in open dialogue. When

28 Judy McGregor, Sylvia Bell and Margaret Wilson, *Report: 'Fault Lines: Human Rights in New Zealand'* (Wellington: The New Zealand Law Foundation, 2015).

29 Ruyu Hung, 'Citizenship With/in or Without Lifeworld? A Critical Review of the Contemporary Perspectives of Citizenship', *Policy Futures in Education* 9.2 (2011): 172–182, 172. doi: 10.2304/pfie.2011.9.2.172.

30 Hung, 'Citizenship With/in', 172.

31 Philippa Hunter and Bruce Farthing, 'History Students Voice Their Thinking: An Opening for Professional Conversations', *set Research Information for Teachers* 3 (2009): 52–59.

problematising history pedagogy in initial teacher education, beginning teachers challenged longstanding contextual preferences for standards' aligned conflict histories, and violent contexts of school history.[32] They struggled with 'difficult knowledge' and the anxieties that difficult knowledge activates.[33] It is in the spaces of difficult knowledge whereby interest, relevance, and understandings are 'in play' to enable young people's voices to be heard. Just as curriculum is fluid, elusive, and open to interpretation, so too is citizenship, because of the dynamic nature of social issues, social literacies, and digital technologies. Multiple conceptions of citizenship are shifting the focus away from the liberal-democratic ideals of citizen status and the responsibilities a person has to the state. Curriculum implementation of citizenship ideals and practices will struggle to keep pace with savvy young citizens who may reshape our thinking about citizenship, because they are living in the future ... right now!

Bibliography

Abowitz, Kathleen Knight and Jason Harnish. 'Contemporary Discourses of Citizenship'. *Review of Educational Research* 75.2 (2006): 653–690.

Banks, James, A. 'Teaching for Social Justice, Diversity, and Citizenship in a Global World'. *The Educational Forum* 68 (2004): 296–305.

Barr, Hugh, John Graham, Philippa Hunter, Paul Keown and Judith McGee. *A Position Paper: Social Studies in the New Zealand School Curriculum.* Ministry of Education, New Zealand: Social, Physical and Health Education Department, School of Education, Hamilton: University of Waikato, 1997.

Benade, Leon. 'Shaping the Responsible, Successful and Contributing Citizen of the Future: "Values" in the New Zealand Curriculum and Its Challenge to the Development of Ethical Teacher Responsibility'. *Policy Futures in Education* 9.2 (2011): 151–162. doi: 10.2304/pfie.2011.9.2.151.

Britzman, Deborah. *Lost Subjects, Contested Objects. Toward a Psychoanalytic Inquiry into Learning.* New York: State University of New York Press, 1998.

Brown, Dave F. 'It's the Curriculum, Stupid! There's Something Wrong with It'. *Contemporary Readings in Curriculum,* edited by Barbara Slater Stern and Marcella L. Kysilka, 291–298. London: Sage, 2008.

32 Philippa Hunter, 'Problematised History Pedagogy as Narrative Research: Self-Fashioning, Dismantled Voices and Reimaginings in History Education' (PhD Thesis, Waikato University, 2013).

33 Deborah Britzman, *Lost Subjects, Contested Objects. Toward a Psychoanalytic Inquiry into Learning* (New York: State University of New York Press, 1998).

Durie, Mason. *Te Mana, Te Kawanatanga. The Politics of Maori Self-Determination.* Auckland: Oxford University Press, 1998.

Eisner, Elliot W. 'Questionable Assumptions about Schooling'. *Phi Delta Kappan,* 84.9 (2003): 648–657.

Giroux, Henry, A. 'Disposable Futures: Dirty Democracy and the Politics of Disposability'. *Education and Hope in Troubled Times: Visions of Change for Our Children's World,* edited by H. Svi Shapiro, 223–241. New York: Routledge, 2009.

Hess, Diana. 'Controversial Issues and Democratic Discourse'. *Handbook of Research in Social Studies Education,* edited by Linda Levstik and Cynthia Tyson, 124–136. New York: Routledge, 2008.

Hinchey, Patricia. *Becoming a Critical Educator. Defining a Classroom Identity, Designing a Critical Pedagogy.* New York: Peter Lang, 2004.

Humpage, Louise. 'Talking about Citizenship in New Zealand'. *Kotuitui, New Zealand Journal of Social Sciences* 3 (2008): 121–134.

Hung, Ruyu. 'Citizenship With/in or Without Lifeworld? A Critical Review of the Contemporary Perspectives of Citizenship'. *Policy Futures in Education* 9.2 (2011): 172–182. doi: 10.2304/pfie.2011.9.2.172.

Hunter, Philippa. 'Problematised History Pedagogy as Narrative Research: Self-Fashioning, Dismantled Voices and Reimaginings in History Education'. PhD Thesis, Waikato University, 2013. http://researchcommons.waikato.ac.nz/handle/10289/7741.

Hunter, Phillippa and Bruce Farthing. 'History Students Voice Their Thinking: An Opening for Professional Conversations'. *set Research Information for Teachers* 3 (2009): 52–59.

Kymlicka, Will. *Multicultural Citizenship.* Oxford: Oxford University Press, 1995.

Kincheloe, Joe, L., ed. *Classroom Teaching: An Introduction.* New York: Peter Lang, 2005.

Kincheloe, Joe, L. 'Critical Pedagogy in the Twenty-First Century: Evolution for Survival'. *Critical Pedagogy: Where Are We Now?*, edited by Peter McLaren and Joe L. Kincheloe, 9–43. New York: Peter Lang, 2007.

Lister, Ruth. 'Citizenship: Towards a Feminist Synthesis'. *Feminist Review* 57 (1997): 28–48.

McGregor, Judy, Sylvia Bell and Margaret Wilson. *Report: 'Fault Lines. Human Rights in New Zealand'.* Wellington: The New Zealand Law Foundation, 2015.

Mutch, Carol. 'Citizenship Education: Does It Have a Place in the Curriculum?' *Curriculum Matters* (2005): 49–69.

New Zealand Educational Review Office. *Evaluation at a Glance: Priority Learners in New Zealand Schools.* Wellington: New Zealand Government, 2012. Viewed 1 October 2012. http://ero.govt.nz/National-Reports/Evaluation-at-a-Glance-Priority-Learners-in-New-Zealand-Schools-August-2012.

New Zealand Educational Review Office. *Wellbeing for Young People's Success at Secondary School.* Wellington: New Zealand Government, 2015. Viewed 15 March 2015. http://ero.govt.nz/National-Reports/Wellbeing-for-Young-People-s-Success-at-Secondary-School-February-2015.

New Zealand Government. *ICSS: International Civic and Citizenship Education Study*. Wellington: New Zealand Government, 2008–2012. Viewed 1 November 2012. https://www.educationcounts.govt.nz/publications/series/iccs.

New Zealand Government. 'New Zeeland's Constitution. A Report on a Conversation'. *Constitutional Advisory Panel*. Wellington: New Zealand Government, n.d. Viewed 10 March 2015. http://www.ourconstitution.org.nz/The-Report.

New Zealand Ministry of Education. *The New Zealand Curriculum: For English-Medium Teaching and Learning in Years 1–13*. Wellington: Learning Media, 2007.

New Zealand Ministry of Education. *Belonging and Participating in Society: Building Conceptual Understandings in the Social Sciences* [BCUSS]. Wellington: Ministry of Education, 2008.

New Zealand Ministry of Education. The NZ Curriculum Update: The Publication of *Being Part of Global Communities*. BCUSS Series 15. Wellington: Ministry of Education, 2011.

New Zealand Ministry of Education. The NZ Curriculum Update: The Publication of *Financial Literacy*: BCUSS Series 15. Wellington: Ministry of Education, 2011.

New Zealand Ministry of Education. *Teaching Digital Citizenship*. Wellington: Ministry of Education, nd. Viewed 1 June 2015. http://elearning.tki.org.nz/Teaching/Digital-citizenship#definition.

New Zealand Ministry of Education. *New Zealand Curriculum Guides: Senior Secondary History*. Wellington: Ministry of Education, 2015. Viewed 20 February 2015. http://seniorsecondary.tki.org.nz/Social-sciences/History.

New Zealand Qualifications Authority. Wellington: NZQA, nd. Viewed 2 February 2015. http://www.nzqa.govt.nz/qualifications-standards/qualifications/ncea/subjects/.

Ochoa-Becker, Anna. 'Socialization and Counter Socialization for a Democracy'. *Democratic Education for Social Studies: An Issues-Centred Decision Making Curriculum*, 65–100. New York: Information Age Publishing, 2007.

Orloff, Anne-Shela. 'Gender and the Social Rights of Citizenship: The Comparative Analysis of Gender Relations and Welfare States'. *American Sociological Review* 58.3 (1993): 303–328.

Pearson, David. 'Citizenship, Identity and Belonging: Addressing the Mythologies of the Unitary Nation State in Aotearoa/New Zealand'. *New Zealand Identities: Departures and Destinations*, edited by James Liu, Tim McCreanor and Teresia Teaiwa, 21–37. Wellington: Victoria University Press, 2005.

Rooney, Kevin. 'Citizenship Education: Making Kids Conform', 2007. Viewed 5 September 2014. http://www.spiked-online.com/index.php?/site/printable/4023/.

Royal Society of New Zealand. *Our Futures, Te Pae Tāwhiti: The 2013 Census and New Zealand's Changing Population*. Wellington: Royal Society of New Zealand, 2014. Viewed 10 January 2015. www.royalsociety.org.nz/expert-advice/papers/yr2014/our-futures/. Schiro, Michael. *Curriculum Theory: Conflicting Visions and Enduring Concerns*. London: Sage, 2008.

Schiro, Michael. *Curriculum Theory: Conflicting Visions and Enduring Concerns.* London: Sage, 2008.

Wood, Philippa. 'Citizenship and Participation of Young People in Aotearoa/New Zealand'. MA Thesis, Massey University, 2013.

Students' Understandings of Citizenship and Citizenship Education in Secondary Schools in Chile

Paula Leal Tejeda

Abstract

This chapter provides insights into what secondary school students understand by citizenship and citizenship education in Chile and how the education system, through the curriculum and the school, influence those understandings. It is justified on the grounds of a renewed interest in citizenship in both the international and the Chilean education context. In the case of Chile, this interest was shown in several reforms in education that have been led by the Governments since the return to democracy in 1990, after the dictatorship of Augusto Pinochet. These reforms have considered the need to include more topics related to citizenship education in the educational curriculum, to make it more relevant to a new globalised scenario and to help students become citizens. However, there is a lack of literature that explores these reforms specifically in terms of citizenship education, taking students' views as a priority. This chapter is based on a study undertaken with grade 12 students (the last grade of secondary school) conducted in a city in southern Chile in 2013. This group of students was chosen because the curriculum aims to prepare young people to exercise active citizenship when graduating from school. A case study method was used to address the aims of the research; two secondary schools, one municipalised (public, secular) and one subsidised (private, faith-based), were selected.

Keywords

citizenship – citizenship education – secondary school students – curriculum reform – Chile

1 Introduction

Reflections on citizenship, from Aristotle in Ancient Greece to present day, have been focused on different issues, depending on historical, geographical, cultural, and social context in which the analysis has been developed. In the

© KONINKLIJKE BRILL NV, LEIDEN, 2022 | DOI:10.1163/9789004429253_008

17th century, liberalism proposed all individuals have right to life, liberty, and property[1]; in the 18th century onwards, citizenship has been defined in terms of the relationship between individuals and a particular political community: the nation-state. In Marshall's words, 'citizenship is a status bestowed on those who are full members of a community'.[2] Post-liberal definitions of citizenship seek to overcome the barriers of liberal definitions and include ideas from socialism, republicanism, communitarianism, feminism and ecologism, amongst others. Rights and responsibilities are mutually supportive and, as Crick argues, from communitarian and civic republican positions being a full citizen necessarily entails active participation in the political community. This participation is given mainly by the right to vote.[3]

Citizenship as a membership to a nation-state has been discussed over the years, since the delimitation of the concept to only a relationship citizenry-state would leave out issues such as identity, belonging to a community and participation of individuals and groups in that community.[4] It also leaves out the current scenario of globalisation and multiculturalism which 'are testing the capacity of nation-states to coordinate and define the collective lives of their citizens, altering the very character of citizenship along the way'.[5] In a (neoliberal) globalised context, citizenship is often related to human capital ideas, i.e., citizens help to build a knowledge-based economy in which economic development and human well-being are crucial.[6] It is in this context that the cosmopolitan orientation of citizenship is valuable to overcome some of the limitations of an understanding of citizenship only as a political affiliation. The cosmopolitan orientation states that 'all individuals are said to be equal ... because of their status as human beings, rather than according to any status ascribed to them as members of an identity set'.[7]

1 Keith Faulks, *Citizenship* (Oxon: Taylor and Francis, 2013), 162.

2 Thomas Marshall, *Citizenship and Social Class* (London: Pluto Press, 1992), 18.

3 Bernard Crick, *A Note on What Is and What Is Not Active Citizenship* (London: LSDA, 2002), np, viewed 10 April 2015. https://www.academia.edu/4443881/A_NOTE_ON_WHAT_IS_AND_WHAT_IS_NOT_ACTIVE_CITIZENSHIP.

4 Sami Zubaida, 'Contests of Citizenship: A Comment', *Citizenship Studies* 3.3 (1999): 387–388.

5 Richard Bellamy, 'Introduction: The Importance and Nature of Citizenship', *Citizenship*, by Richard Bellamy and Antonino Palumbo (Farnham: Ashgate, 2010), xi-xv.

6 Nick Zepke, 'Three Perspectives on Active Citizenship in Lifelong and Life-Wide Education Research', *Lifelong Learning in Europe* (Finland: The Finnish Lifelong Learning Foundation), np, viewed 10 April 2015, http://lline.fi/cn/article/research/220132/three-perspectives-on-active-citizenship-in-lifelong-and-life-wide-education-research.

7 Luis Cabrera, *The Practice of Global Citizenship* (Cambridge: Cambridge University Press, 2014), 14.

In summary, citizenship is a contested concept, though it is relatively consensual that citizenship is a desirable thing.[8] Also, it is agreed that education plays a crucial role in the development of citizenship.[9] UNESCO states that 'citizenship education can be defined as educating children, from early childhood, to become clear-thinking and enlightened citizens who participate in decisions concerning society'.[10] David Kerr defines it as follows:

> … A practice to equip students with a set of tools (knowledge and understanding, skills and attitudes, values and dispositions) which enable them to participate actively and sensibly in the roles and responsibilities they encounter in their adult lives.[11]

In my study, I understand the citizenship education as a practice carried out by schools through particular curriculum subjects and activities aimed at delivering knowledge about citizenship and promoting the development and exercise of citizenship in students.

2 The Context of My Study

This study is justified on the grounds of a renewed interest in citizenship in both the international and the Chilean educational context.[12] This interest is evidenced by education reforms led by the 'Concertación de Partidos por la Democracia' Governments in Chile from 1990 until 2010 after the dictatorship of Augusto Pinochet (1973–1990).[13] These reforms aimed at increasing

---

8 Faulks, *Citizenship*, 171.

9 UNESCO, 'Citizenship Education for the 21st Century', *Teaching and Learning for a Sustainable Future* (United Nations Educational, Scientific and Cultural Organization, 2010), np, viewed 20 April 2015, http://www.unesco.org/education/tlsf/mods/theme_b/mod07.html?panel=2#top.

10 UNESCO, 'Citizenship Education', np.

11 David Kerr, *Citizenship Education: An International Comparison* (Slough: National Foundation for Educational Research, 1999), np, viewed 5 April 2015, https://www.nfer.ac.uk/research/centre-for-information-and-reviews/inca/TS%20Citizenship%20Education%20an%20International%20Comparison%201999.pdf.

12 Bellamy, 'Introduction', xi.

13 The 'Concert of Parties for Democracy' is a coalition of centre-left political parties in Chile founded in 1988 in opposition to the dictatorship of Augusto Pinochet (1973–1990). Presidential candidates from this coalition won every election from when the dictatorship ended in 1990 until the conservative candidate Sebastián Piñera won the Chilean presidential election in 2010.

quality and equality in education, which is essential for developing citizens and human capital.[14] One of the reforms was the enactment of a new curriculum for primary and secondary schools in 1998, which formed the bases for updates in 2005 and 2009 and a new proposal currently being designed and implemented (Curriculum Bases 2013). It establishes fundamental objectives oriented to the competencies or capabilities that students should achieve by the end of secondary education.[15]

Chile has participated in some major international studies, such as the Civic Education Study (CIVED) in 1999 and the International Civic and Citizenship Education Study (ICCS) between 2006 and 2010.[16] These studies show the knowledge that students have in civic matters. However, research on the following specific topics have been largely ignored in Chile: (a) students' views of citizenship education and how it is taught; (b) what secondary school students who are ready to graduate understand by citizenship; (c) the role schools play in the development and practice of citizenship; (d) whether the intended and implemented curriculum is helping or hindering the exercise of citizenship. Considering this lack of literature, my research intends to address how citizenship and citizenship education are discursively constituted in selected municipalised (public) and subsidised (private) schools in Chile. My study is relevant because it contributes to the debate on what concepts and practices of citizenship are being taught in schools, taking the voices of students into consideration as a priority – meaning, what they understand, identify and value.

3 Research Methods

I used an interpretive approach as I attempt to understand phenomena through accessing the meanings participants assign to them, i.e. to place students' understandings of citizenship and citizenship education at the centre

14 Gilbert Valverde, 'Curriculum Convergence in Chile: The Global and Local Context of Reforms in Curriculum Policy', *Comparative Education Review* 48.2 (2004): 177–178.

15 Ministerio de Educación de Chile, *Marco Curricular de la Educación Media. Objetivos Fundamentales y Contenidos Minimos Obligatorios* (Santiago: Unidad de Curriculum y Evaluación del Ministerio de Educación de Chile, 1998), 7.

16 The International Civic and Citizenship Education Study (ICCS) is the largest international study on civic and citizenship education ever conducted. It is carried out by the International Association for the Evaluation of Educational Achievement (IEA), an independent, international cooperative of national research agencies, which, for over 50 years, has conducted large-scale comparative studies of educational achievement and reported on key aspects of educational systems and processes.

of the study.[17] I used a case study method; two secondary schools in southern Chile were chosen, with twenty students in total, ten from each school. They were at grade 12 of secondary school, so most were 17 years old and ready to graduate.

I used several data collection techniques such as document analyses of three versions of the Chilean curriculum: Curriculum 1998, Curriculum Update 2009 and Curriculum Proposal 2013; focus group sessions with students; in-depth interviews with students, heads of schools, teachers and parents and non-participant observation. In this chapter, I am focusing the discussion on findings from the analyses of the curricula and focus group sessions with students. Two focus group sessions were conducted, one in each school, comprising ten students, five females and five males. The discussion was divided into four parts, with topics that covered opinions and thoughts about citizenship, the teaching of citizenship education and a discussion of the role of the school in helping/hindering the practice of citizenship.

The analysis of documents were focused on descriptions, definitions, emphasis and comparisons between versions of the educational curricula. Focus group sessions were recorded and transcribed, and subsequently a coding scheme was developed taking into account concepts, meanings and opinions that were recognised to be most important for students. This information was afterwards grouped into categories of similar meaning, allowing for the definition of categories and subcategories for study.

4 Analysis of Chilean Education Curricula

The three versions of the curricula do not consider the teaching of content on citizenship through one specific subject. Main objectives of the Curriculum 1998 in relation to citizenship are national identity, democracy, contribution to social cohesion and the education of a rational, tolerant citizen, able to understand the past and present and make plans for the future. Decree 220 states: 'Secondary education provides training for the full exercise of citizenship'.[18] It is understood as a *value* and categorised into the *individual* level.[19] In the Update 2009, contents of citizenship are included in History, Geography

17 Wanda Orlikowski and Jack Baroudi, 'Studying Information Technology in Organizations: Research Approaches and Assumptions', *Information Systems Research* 2.1 (1991): 5.

18 Ministerio de Educación de Chile, *Marco Curricular*, iv.

19 Ibid.

and Social Sciences (HGSC) and Philosophy and Psychology subjects. It focuses more on belonging to a civic community in which citizens should participate actively. The Curriculum Bases 2013 proposes to work contents of citizenship from grade 7 in three subjects. Citizenship education is understood as a goal itself rather than a result or outcome of the education process and it incorporates competencies that students need to develop.[20]

I identify several ideologies embedded in the curricula, the main ones being conservative/republican, liberal and neoliberal. Also, human capital theories have influenced the curriculum content. Conservative and neoliberal ideologies are more orientated to keeping the status-quo and relations of power, domination and exploitation.[21] Liberal ideologies aim at social transformation while respecting political order and democracy, and holding individual rights as a priority.[22] Human capital theories focus on work and economic well-being.[23]

The Curriculum 1998 was enacted in a new scenario of democracy, in which a consensus from different political actors was needed to achieve this enactment.[24] Thus, it contains ideologies that represent those actors. The conservative/republican ones aimed at promoting transmission of traditions in a society, loyalty to the state, patriotism, national identity, national history and respect for the homeland. Liberal ideologies are embedded in emphasis on democracy, individual rights, exercise and respect for human rights, and neoliberal ideas in economic growth and the importance of the market, among others. Students need to acquire competencies for success in a globalised world in which entrepreneurship is needed (human capital emphasis). There are a few references to dictatorship, violation of human rights and restructuring of the political and economic order – ideologies sustained by actors from left-wing political parties. Even when there have been slight changes in the following versions of the curricula years 2009 and 2013, it can be argued that these ideologies remain embedded in it.

20 Ministerio de Educación de Chile, *Bases Curriculares 7° y 8° Básico – 1° y 2° Medio* (Santiago: Unidad de Curriculum y Evaluación del Ministerio de Educación de Chile, 2013), 1.

21 Norman Fairclough, *Analysing Discourse. Textual Analysis for Social Research* (London: Routledge, 2003), 218.

22 Faulks, *Citizenship*, 164.

23 Zepke, *Three Perspectives*, np.

24 Cristián Cox and María Lemaitre, 'Market and State Principles of Reform in Chilean Education: Policies and Results', *Chile Recent Policy Lessons*, eds. Guillermo Perry and Danny Leipziger (Washington, D.C.: World Bank Institute, 1999), 149–188.

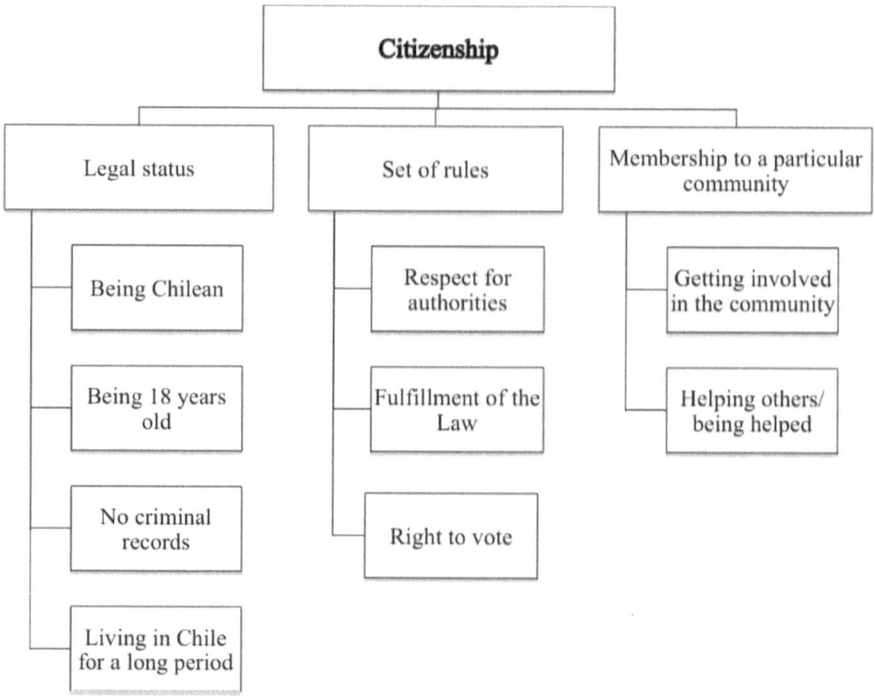

FIGURE 1 Students' understandings of citizenship in secondary schools in Chile
SOURCE: AUTHOR, 2015

5 Focus Groups Findings

No important differences were found between students' understandings of citizenship. They define it in terms of *legal status*, which implies: being Chilean, being 18 years old, not having a criminal record, living in a city/community/country/society and having the right to vote (liberal and social citizenship). Also, citizenship is understood as a commitment to the local community and to actions and behaviours a citizen should show, such as sharing with others, helping others, contributing to the community, contributing to the development and growth of the country, accepting and respecting others and being accepted by other citizens (liberal, conservative views of citizenship), among others. I state that their definitions are more related to how a citizen *should be* and what he or she *should do* rather than what citizens *are* and *do*. The following images summarise students' understandings of citizenship:

I identify differences in how students understand the concept of 'citizen'. Both groups define themselves as individuals who are not citizens yet mainly

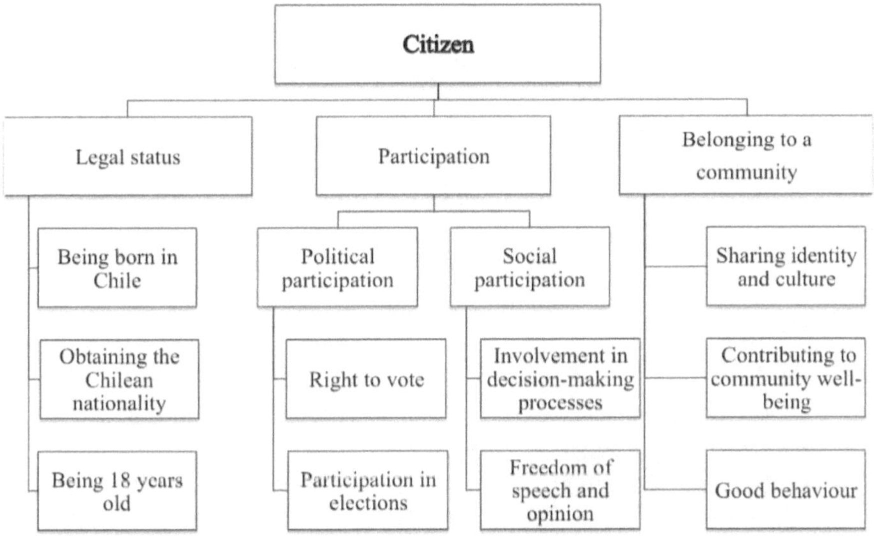

FIGURE 2 Students' understandings of citizen in secondary schools in Chile
SOURCE: AUTHOR, 2015

because they are not of age, i.e. they will become *full* citizens once they turn 18. However, students from the private school think they are citizens in several ways because they are practising their citizenship through school and community involvement. Students' views on citizen from both schools are summarised in the following image:

Almost all students from both schools think that being born and raised in a small city in southern Chile, even when it lacks social and cultural opportunities, have allowed them to develop a sense of belonging to a specific community with differentiated characteristics and in which they have more opportunities to get involved in helping others at the local level. At the same time, they express a sense of isolation because they feel that authorities ignore them.

I found relevant differences in their opinions about the school they attend. Students from the municipalised one (public) express that it is not the best educational institution in the city, though it offers acceptable quality in education. By contrast, students from the subsidised school (private) think it is the best one in the city and, accordingly, have a strong sense of belonging to it. Both groups converge in the recognition of school as an important space that gives them opportunities to participate in extracurricular activities, especially within the community.

Regarding citizenship education, both groups of students agree on the need for a particular subject in which all topics related to citizenship should be covered, such as voting, good civic behaviour, rights, responsibilities and duties and good social behaviour, amongst others. One of the differences between groups is that participants from the public/secular schools identify topics of citizenship being taught mainly in HGSC subject, whereas those from the private/faith-based school mentioned several contents they relate to citizenship and the subjects in which those are being covered (HGSC, Philosophy, Language and Technology).

6 Discussion

I was expecting to find gaps between the students' understanding of citizenship and citizenship education. Even when students share similar definitions of these concepts, the differences are in terms of how they think they are exercising opportunities to become full citizens in the near future and on the role of the school in facilitating the practice of citizenship. I have found that those gaps exist because the subsidised school is a faith-based education institution and not because one is public (municipalised) and the other one private. The school climate of these two schools influences the ways in which students practice their citizenship. In the case of the faith-based school, there is a strong emphasis on the importance of each curriculum subject to help them to become good citizens. Also, a discourse of commitment to the school community and the city where they live: the 'spiritual, the moral and the social are necessarily interconnected as categories'.[25] Thus, perceptions of the exercise of citizenship are different between the two groups. In the view of one student:

> I like my school because we always find opportunities to learn how to be a good citizen. For example, my family and I visit the nursing home a few times a year ... this is a Catholic school, we are supposed to care for others.[26]

It can be argued that although students from the subsidised school establish relationships between being a citizen and exercising citizenship, a relatively large proportion of them do not link knowledge and practices to what is being learned in specific subjects. The evidence shows that a similar situation occurs with students from the municipalised school. Citizenship education is

25 Gerald Grace, 'Educational Studies and Faith-Based Schooling: Moving from Prejudice to Evidence-Based Argument', *British Journal of Educational Studies* (2003), 155.

26 Rosa, student participant from the subsidised school.

understood as a subject in which they should learn civic contents and not as a practice they could experience in more than one subject. Students recognise they are experiencing citizenship through some activities organised by the school even if they do not have a specific subject to learn about it:

> The students' council is important, I always vote for the most honest classmate to be our president. At least I have learnt how to vote, it's funny, it is almost the same when you elect your mayor ... we haven't had any class yet in which we learn how to vote, but we have the students' election, that's good.[27]

Another gap I have found is between where the curricula in the three versions analysed stand in terms of ideologies and definitions of citizenship and citizenship education and specific objectives and examples of the exercise of citizenship. As already mentioned, there has been a slight shift in ideologies within the curriculum. However, what remains the same is the focus on the *individual* who has rights (liberal ideologies) and who needs to develop the knowledge, skills/abilities and attitudes to respond to different contexts both nationally and internationally and the absence of a global dimension of citizenship. That is to say, human capital ideas are embedded in the curricula.

One explanation of why ideologies embedded in the curricula have remained almost the same after the dictatorship of Pinochet is that each version states that it is important to elaborate a new curriculum keeping the bases the previous one has left and building new concepts and content that respect the work done before.[28] Another explanation is that the actors involved in the enactment of the curriculum have historically belonged to groups that align with the main ideologies discussed in this chapter.

The three versions of the curricula state what a citizen *should be* but not what a citizen *is*. Students are being taught that they will be ready to fully exercise their citizenship once they are 18 years old. The discourse is not saying *you already are citizens*. Thus, there is a lack of mention of all the personal, family and community resources students already have that contribute to the current practice of citizenship and all those skills, abilities and attitudes they have developed that constitute them as citizens no matter what their age is. Students are being constructed as passive individuals in need of someone, in

27 Vicente, student participant from the municipalised school.

28 Ministerio de Educación de Chile, *Bases Curriculares*, 1.

this case, the education system, to give them the knowledge to become citizens but not as active citizens who are exercising citizenship.

The curriculum discourse is not related to social groups (specifically groups of students) exercising citizenship. Concepts about teamwork, own initiative, engagement to family, school and community, solving problems and others are related to a point of view of *individuals* developing skills and getting engaged with others in the exercise of citizenship but not of *groups* of human beings practising it. Groups of people organised to achieve goals that contribute to a better society have more power than individuals trying to change certain situations, especially those unequal. One example mentioned during the development of focus groups was the students' mobilisation in Chile.[29] Demonstrations are seen as an opportunity to engage in social demands, but students do not link them to a *movement of citizens*:

> It was fun going out to the main square in town to protest … we carried placards saying "we want better education". But most of us did it just because all students in Chile were doing the same … and because Mauricio (president of the student council) is our friend. Just a small group of us participated, the rest decided to stay at home. We know we live in a small town, and no one hears us, even the Municipality ignores us, there's nothing they can do. If we were in Santiago everything would be different.[30]

The question is how the curriculum could help students reflect on and recognise themselves as citizens and their practices of citizenship as knowledge they have already learned throughout their lifetime, both in the community and the school. One response is a curriculum that links theories, ideologies and experiences of citizenship with what the country envisions as a citizen, and a discourse that emphasises the students' lived experience of citizenship. Actors that could represent different spaces within the society should participate in the enactment of this curriculum. Also, a citizenship education that is not only focused on knowledge, skills and attitudes that individuals should develop but

29 The students' mobilisation during the 2011 is a series of nationwide demonstrations by university and secondary schools students from May to November 2011. This mobilisation aimed to demand from the government a profound educational reform that ensures equality and free education for all. Even when mobilisations are on-going, those that occurred in 2011 are considered the most important demonstrations of recent years and one of the largest since the return to democracy.

30 Eduardo, student participant from the municipalised school.

on social and group interactions that help the practice of citizenship. Finally, I argue that students *are* citizens even when they are not of age. The legal status is one of the dimensions of citizenship, but this does not limit a student to exercise citizenship in all other ways. They are seeking to become more active citizens, and the school is a natural space that helps them to achieve this goal.

Bibliography

Bellamy, Richard. 'Introduction: The Importance and Nature of Citizenship'. *Citizenship*, by Richard Bellamy and Antonino Palumbo, xi–xv. Farnham: Ashgate, 2010.

Cabrera, Luis. *The Practice of Global Citizenship*. Cambridge: Cambridge University Press, 2014.

Cox, Cristián and María Lemaitre. 'Market and State Principles of Reform in Chilean Education: Policies and Results'. *Chile Recent Policy Lessons,* edited by Guillermo Perry and Danny Leipziger Washington, D.C.: World Bank Institute, 1999: 149–188.

Crick, Bernard. *A Note on What Is and What Is Not Active Citizenship*. London: LSDA, 2002. Viewed 10 April 2015. https://www.academia.edu/4443881/A_NOTE_ON_WHAT_IS_AND_WHAT_IS_NOT_ACTIVE_CITIZENSHIP.

Fairclough, Norman. *Analysing Discourse. Textual Analysis for Social Research.* London: Routledge, 2003.

Faulks, Keith. *Citizenship.* Oxon: Taylor and Francis, 2013.

Grace, Gerald. 'Educational Studies and Faith-Based Schooling: Moving from Prejudice to Evidence-Based Argument'. *British Journal of Educational Studies* (2003): 149–167.

Kerr, David. *Citizenship Education: An International Comparison*. Slough: National Foundation for Educational Research, 1999. Viewed 5 April 2015. https://www.nfer.ac.uk/research/centre-for-information-and-reviews/inca/TS%20Citizenship%20Education%20an%20International%20Comparison%201999.pdf.

Marshall, Thomas. *Citizenship and Social Class*. London: Pluto Press, 1992.

Ministerio de Educación de Chile. *Marco Curricular de la Educación Media. Objetivos Fundamentales y Contenidos Minimos Obligatorios*. Santiago: Unidad de Curriculum y Evaluación del Ministerio de Educación de Chile, 1998.

Ministerio de Educación de Chile, *Bases Curriculares 7° y 8° Básico – 1° y 2° Medio.* Santiago: Unidad de Curriculum y Evaluación del Ministerio de Educación de Chile, 2013.

Orlikowski, Wanda and Jack Baroudi. 'Studying Information Technology in Organizations: Research Approaches and Assumptions'. *Information Systems Research* 2.1 (1991): 1–28.

UNESCO. 'Citizenship Education for the 21st Century'. *Teaching and Learning for a Sustainable Future.* United Nations Educational, Scientific and Cultural

Organization, 2010. Viewed 20 April 2015. http://www.unesco.org/education/tlsf/mods/theme_b/mod07.html?panel=2#top.

Valverde, Gilbert. 'Curriculum Convergence in Chile: The Global and Local Context of Reforms in Curriculum Policy'. *Comparative Education Review* 48.2 (2004): 174–201.

Zubaida, Sami. 'Contests of Citizenship: A Comment'. *Citizenship Studies* 3.3 (1999): 387–390.

Zepke, Nick. 'Three Perspectives on Active Citizenship in Lifelong and Life-Wide Education Research'. *Lifelong Learning in Europe*. Finland: The Finnish Lifelong Learning Foundation, 2013. Viewed 10 April 2015. http://lline.fi/en/article/research/220132/three-perspectives-on-active-citizenship-in-lifelong-and-life-wide-education-research.

Why a Third Culture Kid Should Never Be Asked 'Where Are You From?'

Judith Zangerle

Abstract

Today's mobile and highly globalised world has created groups of people who have grown up inside multiple, often initially foreign, cultures. Such people frequently (invisibly) struggle with a confused sense of identity due to personal histories, which often involve transitions, grief and the struggle to fit in. These 'new' citizens, or identities, are on the rise and should therefore, not be overlooked.

Intensive research conducted at a European school in 2012 served as a starting point for this chapter. It was carried out among 'Third Culture Kids' with various cultural and social backgrounds, concentrating on their perception of friendship in relation to their cultural backgrounds. Much of what came up during that research could not be pursued the way I wanted. After all the interesting discoveries I made during my involvement with the children and the analysis of the topic, this chapter calls to attention these new identities by focusing on the roots of their often seemingly confused sense of identity. It provides information on bi- and multiculturalism and particularly, 'Third Culture Kids'. It will also outline what roles globalisation, transition and losses play in the life of an (Adult) Third Culture Kid. Using personal interviews and encounters, firsthand accounts will be presented within the chapter. This chapter hopes to contribute to a wider acknowledgment and awareness of this 'lost generation', and bring to attention a whole group of 'citizens' who, in many cases, have fallen between the cracks.

Keywords

Third Culture Kids – transition – globalisation – home – grief – multiculturalism – culture

1 Bi- and Multiculturalism and Intercultural Interaction

Most of us find it easy to answer the question 'Where are you from?', but not everyone does. Many of us do not belong (or sometimes do not feel like we

© KONINKLIJKE BRILL NV, LEIDEN, 2022 | DOI:10.1163/9789004429253_009

belong) to only one culture or country; many of us are bi- or multicultural and some of us are (Adult) Third Culture Kids. A Third Culture Kid is a child who has spent a 'significant part of his or her developmental years outside the parents' culture'.[1] These new 'citizens' face struggles growing up and into adulthood.

A bicultural person can be defined as someone who 'lives in two or more cultures, who adapts to each and who blends aspects of both'.[2] Bicultural people may be, for example, refugees, immigrants, international students, expatriates, children from bi- or multicultural homes. We have to acknowledge that some people are influenced by this biculturalism more than others. Some features that characterize a bi- or multicultural person are: (a) 'they live in two or more cultures; (b) they adapt, at least in part, to these cultures; and (c) they blend various aspects of the different cultures'.[3] Bicultural people 'have the ability to switch between cultural schemas, norms, and behaviours in response to cultural cues in any given situation'.[4] This ability is often connected to intercultural interaction, which is the interaction between two or more cultures. Other terms for intercultural interaction include 'pluralism', 'the exchange of cultural norms', and 'the process of constructing relationships between cultures'.[5]

2 Being More Than Bi- or Multicultural: Being a Cross / Third Culture Kid

A person's early childhood has a great influence on his/her subsequent life. In my opinion, it is therefore very important to look at the bi- or multicultural children and adolescents in our society who were most influenced by 'cultural schemas, norms, and behaviours'; especially those children and adolescents who can respond appropriately to the cultural cues of cultures that they belong to or live in. These cultures can be the parents' cultures, the residence's culture or any other culture the children are in contact with. Such children and

1 David C. Pollock and Ruth E. Van Reken, *Third Culture Kids* (Boston: Nicholas Brealey Pub, 2009), 13.
2 Paul Pedersen, *Multiculturalism as a Fourth Force* (Philadelphia, Pa: Brunner/Mazel, 1999), 127.
3 Ibid, 127.
4 Paul R. Smokowski and Martica Bacallao, *Becoming Bicultural* (New York: New York University Press, 2010), 11.
5 Jean-Michel, Leclerq, *Facets of Interculturality in Education* (Strasbourg: Council of Europe Publishing, 2003), viewed 13 April 2015, http://www.peacepalacelibrary.nl/ebooks/files/Coe18.pdf.

adolescents can be referred to as Cross Culture Kids, a term introduced by Ruth and her husband John Useem in the 1950s.

Cross Culture Kids (CCK) can be:

- Children from bi- or multicultural homes, where parents might have a bi- or multicultural background themselves
- Children of immigrants
- Educational CCKs: Children who may remain in their home or passport country but are sent to a school of a different culture or cultures (e.g. an international school)
- Children of refugees
- Children who cross borders frequently
- Children of minorities: Children whose parents are from a racial or ethnic group that is not part of the majority race or ethnicity in the country in which they live
- International adoptees
- Domestic CCKs: Children whose parents have moved in or among various subcultures within that child's home country.[6]

Many CCKs can belong to more than one category. The term 'Global nomads' is often used to describe the same individuals, where the parents' occupation plays a more vital role within this definition. This will be discussed in greater detail shortly.

We can also find other terms for the same individuals, such as 'internationally mobile children or adolescents'[7] and 'trans-cultural or transitional children'.[8] The existence of these terms demonstrates, I would argue, that there are enough people now in this situation for a need for special phrases to describe them.

Another term, within the world of a CCK, that the Useems address is the definition of a Third Culture Kid (TCK). A TCK is somehow a subcategory of CCKs, but can also be seen as an overarching term, depending on the viewpoint. The Useems define a TCK as one who has spent a 'significant part of his or her developmental years outside their parents' culture'.[9] It is important to see the different cultures a TCK is surrounded by as a fusion of cultures. The

6 Ibid., 32.

7 Michael, Gerner, et. al., 'Characteristics of Internationally Mobile Adolescents'. *Journal of School Psychology* 30.2 (1992): 197–214.

8 David B. Willis, 'Transculturals, Transnationals: The New Diaspora' *International Schools Journal*, XIV, 1, 29–42 as quoted in Ettie, Zilber, *Third Culture Kids: The Children of Educators in International Schools: John Catt Educational.* (Glasgow: Bell and Bain, 2009), 37.

9 Pollock and Van Reken, *Third Culture Kids*, 13.

Useems, and later in more detail Pollock and Van Reken, define the first culture of a TCK as the culture of the country from which the parents originated. The second culture refers to the culture in which the family currently resides. Alas, TCKs often live in a sort of no-man's land: 'neither the world of their parents' culture (or cultures) nor fully the world of the other culture (or cultures) in which they were raised'.[10] They do not always have a lot of contact with the home culture of their parents and may only ever visit that country on holiday. 'It's hard because belonging is often tied to home. And home is ever-changing and ever-moving'.[11]

As a result, a new almost invisible culture is introduced into the life of a TCK. This invisible bond can be called the *'Third Culture'*, a fusion of two first (parent's and residence) cultures.[12]

The TCK term is a common enough term and widely used among children, adolescents and also adults who refer to themselves as such and can finally "define" themselves, as I have found out during many interviews with TCKs.

Despite the fact that children who live in this sort of no-man's land might have little in common, it is this third culture that unites them. One of the participants I spoke to says, '[M]y parents just happened to move to different countries. And I think we'll only truly belong among other Third Culture Kids'.[13]

Even though TCKs may have many rich and varied cultural experiences, they face a lot of difficulties and challenges. In particular, for TCKs who move around frequently, high mobility often contributes to a huge number of relationships 'with people throughout the world, but it also creates sadness at the chronic loss of these relationships'.[14]

3 Globalisation and Transition

A child can become a TCK in various ways. Due to today's mobile workplace, many parents move around frequently to pursue their careers. Often, we find such parents in the diplomatic corps, military, international business, or

10 Ibid, 4.
11 Michele Phoenix, 'Introduction to MKs (and TCKs)', *YouTube*, 10 February 2010, Viewed on 13 April 2015, https://bit.ly/2FoxE4z .
12 Pollock and Van Reken, *Third Culture Kids*, 14.
13 C.C., in discussion with the author, May 2011.
14 Pollock and Van Reken, *Third Culture Kids*, 87.

working as missionaries. The 'experience of growing up in a profoundly culturally mixed environment is becoming increasingly common'.[15]

This phenomenon introduces new possibilities and aspects that have a bearing on human beings – and especially on children who – by choice or not – are highly affected as a result of globalisation. Because of such a nomadic lifestyle, many TCKs and Adult TCKs find it very difficult to define 'home'. According to Pollock and Van Reken,:

> Like nomads, we moved with the seasons. Four times a year, we packed up and moved to, or back to, another temporary home. As with the seasons, each move offered something to look forward while something had to be given up ... We learned early that 'home' was an ambiguous concept, and wherever we lived, some essential part of our lives was always someplace else. So we were always of two minds. We learned to be happy and sad at the same time. We learned to be independent and [accept] that things were out of control.[16]

This quotation is a good example of the Janus-faced character of a high mobility life. On the one hand, new experiences could be acquired and the journeys along the way are exciting; on the other hand, a certain feeling of security is missing, and things were out of control. As succinctly described by one interview participant, 'I believe that being a TCK has made me 'rich' beyond imagining. It has also pained me more than I can describe'.[17]

> '... mostly I just think of it [being a TCK] as a curse. My life right now is so agonizingly fragmented. I've lost my sense of self, feel like an anomaly/ misfit in every group and am struggling with depression. But at the same time, if given the choice, I don't think I would exchange my life for a less mobile one. It's made me who I am, adding deeper dimensions to the way I think and the way I perceive the world'.[18]

In addition to the many experiences one acquires during the stages of high mobility, every one of us goes through some type of transition throughout life. For people who are not TCKs or who are not especially mobile, many transitions brought on by mobility are expected and therefore planned in advance,

15 Ibid., 28.
16 Ibid., 65.
17 C.C., in discussion with the author, May 2011.
18 M.E., e-mail message to Author, February, 28, 2010.

although some do of course happen unexpectedly. Concerning a TCK's experience of mobility, the transition is in context with the physical movement which TCKs experience a lot – and they usually experience it emotionally unprepared.

Pollock and Van Reken created a model of transition.[19] The model consists of five phases, each phase pointing out how one is perceived by others (social status), how one presents one's self to and interacts with others (social posture) and how one typically feels inside (psychological and emotional experience). I will briefly address the main features of each phase:

1. Involvement

At this stage, one feels at home where he/she is living. One has the feeling that he/she has settled down and this makes him/her feel comfortable and secure.

2. Leaving

Right after one finds out that he/she will be moving and therefore leaving, he/she enters this stage. Detachment is normal but can 'produce anger and frustration in relationships that have been close'.[20] Additionally, the feeling of denial arises, one 'unconsciously [tries] to make the leaving as painless'[21] as possible. Denial is at the core of this stage. One begins to put an emotional distance between him/herself and friends. When one informs his/her friends that he/ she is moving again, the bonds of group belonging are loosened. He/she will be excluded from group events taking place after he/she leaves and a feeling of rejection ensues.

'Having to say goodbye all the time doesn't mean it gets easier. It just gets more'.[22]

3. Transition

This stage begins with the very moment one leaves his/her country. It is a 'time of uncertainty, a time of entering the unknown, and is usually characterized by chaos, stress, and anxiety'.[23] A strong feeling of loss can occur and one is likely to take stock of oneself. Disappointment and low self-esteem often result from not knowing how to fit into the new culture.

19 Pollock and Van Reken, *Third Culture Kids*, 66–73.
20 Ibid, 67.
21 Ibid., 68.
22 Michele Phoenix, 'Introduction to MKs (and TCKs)'.
23 Eithne, Gallagher, *Equal Rights*, 42.

This makes it even more difficult to overcome the feeling of being new and 'statuslessness'.[24] Often rejection of the new community and its members is the case. This stage only ends when one has finally 'mentally and emotionally decided to engage in the life of the new community'[25] and not with the arrival in the new country, city, or culture. Some people, however, 'never fully engage in the new location and remain in the transition stage during the entire time they live in another country',[26] as appropriately described by two interview participants:

'I can fit into most contexts, but I don't have one that fits me'[27];

'I understand a lot, I understand people. But I feel misunderstood'.[28]

4. Entering

One starts to accept the situation and is willing to join a new community. New things need to be learned, risks need to be taken, and new information can be gathered. During this stage, feelings can be mixed. On the one hand, one feels delighted and excited about the new impressions. However, on the other hand, a feeling of longing for the old days is still present. Often, 'culture shock and cultural adaption'[29] take place at the same time. Nevertheless, a feeling of security develops, accompanied by an increase in self- confidence. Often this stage is also marked by a 'process of cultural adjustment [... .] followed by culture shock where we feel confused and disoriented in our new surroundings'.[30]

5. Reinvolvement

Full acceptance and the feeling of finally having arrived characterize this stage. People often see themselves as part of a group (again) and the group sees them as a valid member. At this stage, a 'sense of place and belonging in our new community'[31] is dominant.

---

24 Pollock and Van Reken, *Third Culture Kids*,70.

25 Gallagher, *Equal Rights*, 42.

26 Edna, Murphy, *Welcoming Linguistic Diversity in Early Childhood Classrooms* (New York: Multilingual Matters, 2011), 128.

27 Phoenix, 'Introduction to MKs (and TCKs)'.

28 Ibid.

29 Murphy, *Welcoming*, 128.

30 Gallagher, *Equal Rights*, 42.

31 Ibid., 42.

4 What Is Left: The Grief and the Loss

> There was no funeral. No flowers. No ceremony. No one had died.
> No weeping or wailing. Just in my heart. *I can't …*
> But I did anyway, and nobody knew I couldn't.
> *I don't want to …*
> But nobody else said they didn't.
> So I put down my panic and picked my luggage and got on the plane.
> There was no funeral.[32]

TCKs and Adult TCKs often experience a strong feeling of grief because of 'the very richness of their lives'.[33] They often have made many acquaintances and friends in the various places they have lived. Despite the fact that having many friends is something they love and makes them different from 'normal' children or also adults, some TCKs have a strong feeling that friendships will not last: 'Saying good-bye is so hard because you know you'll probably never see these people again. You get to the place where you don't want to make friends anymore',[34] but some TCKs also admit that due to their nomadic lifestyle personal ties are more important than anything else: 'At 32 years old, I have realized that my roots are in people, not places. Staying somewhere drains me, starves my inspiration'.[35]

During the different stages of transition, TCKs often face a deep sense of grieving: denial, anger, bargaining, depression/sadness, and acceptance.[36] These are the five stages of grief, which are often connected to the 'loss of a friend, may it be geographically or due to an event of death; but in a way it's a transition process within the overall transition experience'.[37] How intense this process is depends on how intense the loss is. 'I think losses have become something expected and normal in my life'.[38]

For TCKs, this process is sometimes experienced repeatedly, often leading to unresolved grief. There are many different causes for unresolved grief.

---

32 'Mock Funeral', poem by Alex Graham James, quoted in Pollock and Van Reken, 2009,159.

33 Pollock and Van Reken, *Third Culture Kids*, 75.

34 Teresa G., Labov and Carolyn D. Smith. 'The Absentee American: Repatriates' Perspectives on America and Its Place in the Contemporary World'. *International Migration Review* 27 (2): 432, (1993), 71.

35 B. S, in discussion with the author, November 2011.

36 'The Greef Wheel' by Pamela Davis, 2003, quoted in Pollock and Van Reken, 2009, 75.

37 Pollock, Van Reken, *Third Culture Kids*, 74.

38 Phoenix, 'Introduction to MKs (and TCKs)'.

Sometimes, TCKs fear that accepting any painful experiences will lead them to the deny the pleasures that they could have also experienced: 'To admit how sad it was to leave Grandma in the home country feels like a denial of how glad they were to return to their friends in the host country'.[39] Also, hidden losses are omnipresent: loss of their world, of their status (identity), lifestyle, possessions, relationships, role models, and the past, or a past that was more imagined than real. Every hidden loss is related to the 'major human needs we all have of belonging, feeling significant to others and being understood'.[40] It can be the case that TCKs do not really have the permission or at least feel like they do not have the permission to process what has just happened or to express their grief.

> Of course, grief isn't fun. It's not something we love to experience. But it is a reality. Sometimes we're told to 'suck it up' and shake it off, stop feeling sorry for yourself. We're not allowed to fully express our grief. I remember once right after my sister died, my dad and I were sitting together in the house. I was trying really hard to hold back my tears. I thought that my crying would upset my parents all the more, and I didn't want to do that (…) Living the TCK life, my parents didn't understand my grief. How can you be sad? We're in Singapore! We're in London! Look how lucky you are! But they were looking at our life situation from the perspective of a fully formed adult, who has the foundation of their selves fully in place. From my perspective, I was still under construction. It was like someone was stacking coins on top of each other. One quarter on top of the other, evenly spaced. With every move or loss, someone came along and flicked one of the coins out of center, but the stack continued to grow. After that, of course, the stack was unsteady, apt to crumble at any minute. I hadn't lived long enough to have a stable base from which to appreciate the things and places I was seeing. Grieving for a dead sibling is okay. But the grief for my lost friends, my lost homes, was not okay or understandable.[41]

Sometimes, the initially unresolved grief can transform into a kind of delayed grief. The hidden and unresolved issues often hit (Adult) TCKs out of the blue: suddenly they realize that they have suppressed their feelings. Usually

---

39 Pollock, Van Reken, *Third Culture Kids*, 76.

40 Ibid., 80.

41 Elizabeth Evans, 'TCKs and Grief', *Recovered Third Culture Kid*, December 18, 2011, viewed on 28, March, 2015. http://kazakhstanii.blogspot.com.es/2011/12/tcks-and-grief.html (Blog).

this realization occurs 'between the ages of 25 and 40 (...) [and often] when they have their own children, as they start recalling their own childhood and empathizing with their own children'.[42] The grief, however, does not need to remain unresolved. Many TCKs manage to overcome their grief, often with the help of other TCKs.

5 Retrospect

TCKs, with their worries and their exciting lifestyle, are a topic too rich and too broad for this one chapter. Grief, losses, and goodbyes are omnipresent in the life of a TCK and shape it in a way which is difficult to imagine for non-TCKs. Apart from these very substantial downsides, which have been discussed in detail earlier, it is also important to acknowledge that TCKs represent the world's variety. They live a highly cosmopolitan life because they are often surrounded by a 'really free open melting pot of cultures'.[43] Understanding them can enrich our view of our own multicultural societies and its many differences. As citizens of the world and generally open-minded people, TCKs have a certain flexibility towards different cultures and cultural concepts. Not only are they aware of many different concepts, but have often learned to adapt to them. This cross-cultural adaptation has the highly beneficial effect of helping TCK adjust to almost any other cultural environment. We have to try to understand the dynamics a TCK goes through every time he/she is in the state of transition; to try to understand their fears, problems and feelings of rootlessness; and most importantly, to be able to understand '[w]hy a Third Culture Kid should never be asked 'Where are you from?''

Bibliography

Evans, Elizabeth. 'TCKs and Grief'. *Recovered Third Culture Kid*, 18 December, 2011. Viewed on 28 March 2015, http://kazakhstanii.blogspot.com.es/2011/12/tcks-and-grief.html. (Blog).

Gallagher, Eithne. *Equal Rights to the Curriculum*. Clevedon: Multilingual Matters, 2008.

Gerner, Michael, Fred Perry, Mark A. Moselle, and Mike Archbold. 'Characteristics of Internationally Mobile Adolescents'. *Journal of School Psychology* 30.2 (1992): 197–214.

42 Pollock and Van Reken, *Third Culture Kids*, 165.

43 S.L., in discussion with the author, May 2011.

Leclercq, Jean-Michel. *Facets of Interculturality in Education.* (Strasbourg: Council of Europe Publishing, 2003), viewed 13 April 2015, http://www.peacepalacelibrary.nl/ebooks/files/Coe18.pdf.

Jenkins, Richard. *Social Identity* (3rd ed.). London: Routledge, 2008.

Labov, Teresa G., and Carolyn D. Smith. 'The Absentee American: Repatriates. Perspectives on America and Its Place in the Contemporary World'. *International Migration Review* 27 (2): 1993, 432, 71.

Laszloffy, Tracey and Rockquemore, Kerry Ann. *Raising Biracial Children.* Alta Mira: Press, U.S., 2005.

Murphy, Edna. *Welcoming Linguistic Diversity in Early Childhood Classrooms.* New York: Multilingual Matters, 2011.

Pedersen, Paul. *Multiculturalism as a Fourth Force.* Philadelphia, Pa: Brunner/Mazel, 1999.

Pollock, David C., and Ruth E. Van Reken. *Third Culture Kids.* Boston: Nicholas Brealey Pub, 2009.

Rader, Debra, and Linda Harris Sittig. *New Kid in School.* New York: Teachers College Press, 2003.

Rojas, Tanja. 'Hispanic Cultural Values and the Interpersonal Psychotherapy Model for Depression'. PhD Dissertation, Azusa Pacific University, 2008.

Rust, Jonathan P. 'Biculturalism, Cultural Identity, Self Esteem, and Academic Achievement of African-American High School Students'. PhD Dissertation, Fordham University, 2008.

Schaetti, B.F. and Ramsey, S.J. 'The Global Nomad Experience: Living in Liminality'. *Crestone Institute,* 2007. Viewed on 1 April 2015. http://www.transition-dynamics.com/crestone/globalnomad.html.

Shaules, Joseph. *Deep Culture: The Hidden Challenges of Global Living. Languages for Intercultural Communication and Education: Vol. 16.* Clevedon, Buffalo: Multilingual Matters, 2007.

Schreiner, Karin. *Mit der Familie ins Ausland.* Gottingen: Vandenhoeck and Ruprecht, 2009.

Smokowski, Paul R, and Martica Bacallao. *Becoming Bicultural.* New York: New York University Press, 2010.

Spencer-Oatey, Helen, and Peter Franklin. *Intercultural Interaction.* Basingstoke: Palgrave Macmillan, 2009.

Steger, Manfred B. *Globalization.* Toronto: Sterling Publishing Co., Inc., 2010.

Zilber, Ettie. *Third Culture Kids: The Children of Educators in International Schools: John Catt Educational.* Glasgow: Bell and Bain, 2009.

PART 4

Governing Citizenship

Decentralisation and the Identity of the Citizen

Deepening Democracy or Driving Disadvantage?

Tamara Nair

Abstract

It can be argued that one of the principal aims of democratic decentralisation is to promote sustainable development where communities prioritise projects and are closely involved in the planning, and at times even the implementation, of those projects. Such local level participation allows marginalised groups in society to be part of the political process and allows them to exercise their rights as citizens, giving them a legitimate space for greater involvement. However, it has been revealed that decentralised governance does not always benefit marginalised groups and can in some cases symbolise an exercise of power over these disenfranchised communities. Using the state of Kerala as an example, I demonstrate how the pursuit of decentralised governance has had effects on building social capital and ideas of citizenship. Informed by empirical data gathered from fieldwork, furthered by Michel Foucault's ideas on discourse creation and governmentality, I argue that the effects of reservation in India has galvanised disadvantaged groups to be organised as effective proxies through whom existing power dynamics prevail. Ideas of citizenship and its rights become centred on the bodies of the marginalised in society and fail to represent individual rights and freedoms that citizenship encompasses. In deepening the critique of such forms of political inclusion, strategies of deepening democracy and the identity of the citizen has at times served to further marginalise disenfranchised communities.

Keywords

citizenship – decentralisation – Kerala – governmentality

1 Introduction

In the political sphere, sustainable development is best represented by a democratic, broad-based, participatory system where the focus lies on local communities and their empowerment. This is an optimum way to *integrate economic* (equal opportunities of employment and just distribution of wealth),

© KONINKLIJKE BRILL NV, LEIDEN, 2022 | DOI:10.1163/9789004429253_010

social (empowerment, participation and the inclusion of local knowledge) and *environmental* (preservation of biodiversity and protection of natural environments and resources) *spheres*. It can be argued that one of the principal aims of democratic decentralisation is to promote sustainable development where communities prioritise projects and are closely involved in the planning, and at times even the implementation of those projects. Such local level participation allows marginalised groups in society to be part of the political process and allows them to exercise their rights as citizens, giving them a legitimate space for greater involvement. The political will to embark on a sustainable path to growth is most reflected in devolving power, a move from a solely 'top-down' approach to a combination of centrally controlled and 'bottom-up' styles of governance.

Decentralisation is commonly considered a sign of good governance and an equitable path to development. Local government institutions become fundamental in engaging grassroots participation, and the pursuit of a community-based sustainable development requires a political system that ensures effective citizen participation.[1] Using India, the state of Kerala in particular, as a case study, I present how the pursuit of sustainable development, through decentralised governance has had effects on building social capital and ideas of citizenship.

2 An Indian Case Study

Ideas of democracy and citizenship in post-colonial societies such as India are very different from western interpretations of liberal democracy; citizenship is ambiguously placed in democratic ideals.[2] In such societies, there are multiple ways of being thought of as a political entity; the right of political participation of such an entity is attached to more than just being 'a citizen'. It also depends, as in the case of India, on one's class, caste and gender. The 73rd and 74th constitutional amendments, to the Panchayati Raj Act in 1992 gave impetus to the decentralisation process in India.[3] In addition to other stipulations, the Act mandated one third of total number of seats and offices for women and the

1 World Commission on Environment and Development, *Our Common Future* (New York: Oxford University Press, 1987).

2 Nivedita Menon, 'Sexuality, Caste, Governmentality: Contests over "Gender" in India', *Feminist Review* 91 (2009): 96.

3 The term 'panchayat' refers to local government institution. I use the term panchayat interchangeably with local government institutions when referring to India/Kerala.

reservation of seats and offices for India's various scheduled castes and scheduled tribe members, in proportion to their population. The implementation of this devolution of power to local government institutions was left to the states. Some like Kerala and Madhya Pradesh, as Medha Lele states in her work on local governments, have made changes to their own state constitutions, such as the Kerala State Panchayat Raj Act and Madhya Pradesh Gram Swarajya Act,[4] while others have some way to go.

The effects of this reservation have resulted in many members of disadvantaged groups becoming proxy political representatives through which traditional power holders still operate. Ideas of citizenship and accompanying political rights are centred on the bodies of the marginalised and fail to represent individual rights and freedoms that citizenship encompasses. I wish to explore the extent to which decentralised planning has deepened democracy at the grassroots level and has added value to ideas of citizenship. Using a well-established decentralised system as that found in the state of Kerala as a specific case in point, this chapter reveals how decentralised development has created an uneven playing field for certain groups in society despite institutions that have been set up to promote greater equity and representation.

In 2012, I conducted a field study in Kerala over five months. I travelled extensively in the state and managed to speak with local community members as well as members of the tribal and fishing communities (both marginalised groups in Kerala). In addition, I also had a chance to speak with women representatives in the local government, including a panchayat (local government) president, a woman from the Kadar tribal community. Although the data presented here is unique to Kerala, the discussion is relevant to general debates on the role of decentralised governance in building social, natural and economic capital in developing countries and serves up lessons that can be gleaned from the Kerala experience. Decentralised governance in Kerala, initiated as a campaign – the People's Plan for Democratic Decentralisation (henceforth, People's Plan), has also been on-going since 1996, and the time frame of more than two decades makes the state an ideal study of the process.

4 Medha K. Lele, 'Local Government: Conflict of Interests and Issues of Legitimisation', *Economic and Political Weekly* 36 (2001): 4702.

3 The People's Plan in Kerala

Unlike other states in India, Kerala is unique in terms of its famous 'development model'.[5] Despite experiencing consistently lagging economic growth, sharing little in India's economic boom and depending heavily on 'gulf remunerations',[6] the state boasts one of the highest growths in social capital in India, often comparable to that in developed nations. Such accolades notwithstanding, Kerala still witnesses pockets of exclusionary development – marginalised 'outliers',[7] that have failed to be part of the state's social welfare policies and in recent times, its attempts at decentralised sustainable development. An archaeology of caste hierarchy and the status of women reveal how through an 'anatomo-politics of the human body'[8] or disciplinary techniques, and 'regulatory controls; a biopolitics of the population',[9] have created certain expected behaviours through established norms.[10] Today, such norms hamper effective participatory planning. For example, the way the state and mainstream society seem to discredit tribal organisation underscore the way they imagine this community and how they understand tribal discourse.[11] If tribal communities do come 'up in arms' over injustices done to them, this is treated as a one off event as the common belief is that they do not have the capacity to organise in great numbers or have the power as citizens to influence the state.[12]

The number of studies in participatory planning with marginalised communities in the state is small, making it hard to fully evaluate the effectiveness of the People's Plan for those communities. In studies that do exist, there are

---

5 Véron, René. "The "new" Kerala model: Lessons for sustainable development." *World development* 29.4 (2001): 601–617; Parayil, Govindan, and T. T. Sreekumar. "Kerala's experience of development and change." *Journal of Contemporary Asia* 33.4 (2003): 465–492; Kannan, K. P. "Kerala's turnaround in growth: Role of social development, remittances and reform." *Economic and Political Weekly* (2005): 548–554; Oommen, M. A. *Rethinking development: Kerala's development experience.* Vol. 2. New Delhi: Concept publishing company, 1999, among many others.

6 A large number of Malayalees (an Indian ethnic group originating from the state) work overseas (the majority in Gulf countries), sending home money that is channelled into the economy.

7 John Kurien, 'The Kerala Model: Its Central Tendency and the "Outlier"', *Kerala: The Development Experience. Reflections on Sustainability and Replicability*, ed. Govindan Parayil (London and New York: Zed Books, 2000).

8 Michel Foucault, *History of Sexuality* (Victoria Australia; Penguin Group, 2008), 139.

9 Ibid.

10 Tamara Nair, 'Capability and Cultural Subjects: A Reassessment of Power and Social Development in Kerala, India' (PhD diss., University of New South Wales, 2012).

11 Ibid.

12 Ibid.

criticisms of the model,[13] and my field evidence is consistent with this. The fact that studies on development in marginalised communities are limited itself seems characteristic of a process of homogenising Kerala society by emphasising quantifiable general achievements in social development, while keeping discrepancies hidden.

4 Governmentality of Decentralised Development

The Communist Party of India, Marxist (CPM), which formed the largest part of the Left Democratic Front (LDF) coalition government, was the ruling party at the time the People's Plan was launched. The LDF coalition saw itself as a 'vanguard party leading the class struggle and establishing the hegemony of the working class'.[14] The term governmentality, by French philosopher Michel Foucault, can refer to how the state exercises power or governs its population through knowledge (or rationale) and techniques (or methods). For the LDF, decentralisation was based on the rationale of class struggle and the method by which this would be exercised with the People's Plan. Given this ultimate objective, its co-operation with civil society organisations and the opposition parties was for tactical purposes. This in itself is not a new phenomenon or alarming, as it is an oft-employed political strategy. However, such a view (class struggle) on participatory planning as a hallmark of the People's Plan ignores the plurality that exists within the whole democratic process and entrenches existing social interactions.

Pluralism is inherent in democracy, and decentralisation has to support the case for plurality; such homogenisation (all as one in a class struggle) compromises the capabilities (including political rights) of people, to use Amartya Sen's term,[15] especially those that are already marginalised and

13 A. Damodaran, 'Tribals, Forests and Resource Conflicts in Kerala, India: The Status Quo of Policy Change', *Oxford Development Studies* 34.3 (2006); Gail Omvedt, 'Kerala Is Part of India: The Kerala Model of Development, Dalits and Globalisation', *Kerala: The Paradoxes of Public Action and Development*, ed. Joseph Tharamangalam (New Delhi: Orient Longman, 2006); K. Saradamoni, 'Women and the Changed Family in Kerala: Some Masked Realities', *Kerala: The Paradoxes of Public Action and Development*, ed. Joseph Tharamangalam (New Delhi: Orient Longman, 2006), and John Kurien, 'The Kerala Model: Its Central Tendency and the "Outlier"', *Kerala: The Development Experience. Reflections on Sustainability and Replicability*, ed. Govindan Parayil (London and New York: Zed Books, 2000).

14 Joseph Tharamangalam, 'Understanding Kerala's Paradoxes: The Problematic of the Kerala Model of Development', *Kerala: The Paradoxes of Public Action and Development*, ed. by Joseph Tharamangalam (New Delhi: Orient Longman, 2006): 25.

15 Amartya Sen, *Development as Freedom* (New York: Alfred A. Knopf Inc., 2009).

do not have a strong say in the planning process. Effective participation in Kerala then has more to do with the dynamic interplay of politics and civil society. Political patronage is a problem that plagues participatory planning in Kerala. In a way, the amendments to the local government Act gave the state an opening for further involvement, ironically through participatory planning.

With all of the above comes the issue of 'proxy representation'. With reference to a study conducted by Jos Chathukulam and M.S. John[16] and more recent works by M.S. Navaneeth as well as K. Jafar,[17] among others, highlight how women or members of scheduled castes and scheduled tribes are often elected to office under their respective reservation seats end up as mere puppets. Party (usually male, upper caste) members 'rule' through them thus negating the potential effects of mandated representation of disenfranchised groups. Women who are elected also tend to be wives/widows, sisters or even mothers of key male figures in the local community.[18] This is not to say that all women who come into local government through their various party and familial relationships do not do their jobs well. However, the level of such proxy representation warrants concern at how such control influences the lives of the marginalised groups in general and how that redefines their political rights as citizens.

Individual and/or community identities are lost when people are homogenised and the normalised manner in which decisions are made is ignored. The political voice of different groups or individuals disappears when social development policies are driven by ideology that sees all as a 'unified organic whole'.[19] Through proxy representation the individual and the community she / he represents 'vanishes'.

---

16 Chathukulam, Jos, and M. S. John. "Empowerment of women panchayat members: learning from Kerala (India)." *Asian Journal of Women's Studies* 6.4 (2000): 66–101.

17 Navaneeth, M.S. "Reservations for Women in Kerala's Local Self-government Institutions: A Mere Tokenism?" *Working Paper*, Department of Humanities and Social Sciences, IIT Madras (16 May 2020). https://ssrn.com/abstract=3758947; Jafar, K. "Reservation and women's political freedom: Candidates' Experience from three gram panchayats in Kerala, India." *Social Change* 43.1 (2013): 79–97.

18 Navneeth, "Reservations for Women in Kerala's Local Self-government Institutions".

19 Arun Agrawal and Clark, C. Gibson, 'Enchantment and Disenchantment: The Role of Community in Natural Resource Conservation', *World Development* 27 (1999): 633.

5 Concluding Remarks: Changing Ideas of Citizenship and the Way Forward

It can be argued that the effects of reservation have galvanised disadvantaged groups (scheduled castes, scheduled tribes and women) to be organised as effective proxies through whom existing power dynamics prevail. Now their identities become a means for certain benefits, not only for them but for those who see the advantages of 'allowing' them seats in local government. Ideas of citizenship and its rights become connected with group identities (a particular caste, tribe or gender) and fail to represent individual rights and freedoms that citizenship encompasses. Policies that do not promote equitable sustainable development also move towards promoting human insecurities in its various forms since the 'achievement of the development objective defined as the enlargement of human choices is adversely affected by individual/community insecurity because insecurity cuts short life and thwarts the use of human potential'.[20]

Sociologists Molineux and Razavi have gone so far as to say that decentralisation is simply a 'sweetener for the bitter pill of neoliberal adjustment and rising inequality'.[21] Perhaps such a pessimistic view is not necessary. There are several reasons why decentralised governance benefits communities including greater representation and addressing democratic shortfalls. However, there is clearly a pressing need for deliberate reflections on the culture of planning and decision-making in participatory development. What is required is a conscientious effort at closely examining the discourse surrounding local government and citizen engagement *vis-à-vis* disadvantaged groups, hence a stronger call for 'inclusive' participatory development.

Inclusive development should involve putting forth strategies that are formulated with the recipients in mind and then merging those strategies within the larger development framework that should encompass establishing and highlighting the various dimensions of citizenship in India. For example, marginalised tribal and fishing communities in Kerala, as well as women (often from poorer families) become 'projects' within the bigger political discourse. In Kerala, institutions such as *Kudumbashree* (a self-help group for women) or *Vana Samrakshana Samithi* (forest protection councils), a joint venture between the Kerala Forest Department and tribal communities, create a

20 Frances Stewart, 'Development and Security', *Conflict, Security & Development* 4 (2004).

21 Maxine Molineux and Shahrah Razavi, 'Introduction', *Gender Justice, Development and Rights*, ed. Maxine Molyneux and Shahrah Razavi (Oxford: Oxford University Press, 2002), 3–4.

negotiable space within a predominantly patriarchal system that allows their participation but does little in terms of exercising their rights as citizens.[22] This is because they still move within the same playing field, where decisions are made elsewhere and the implementation of those decisions is left with the 'other' to carry out. Genuine inclusion requires active listening on the part of policymakers. Kerala's *gram sabha* (village assembly) and *oorukootam* (tribal village gathering) are excellent fora for this. These institutions, for all their existing failings, present genuine opportunities for integration and, by way of actually listening to what people have to say, a means to promote equality as well.

Education, of course, has been heralded as a great equaliser as well. Kerala is one of the most literate states in India, with literacy levels often above the 90th percentile.[23] Despite the extensive spread of education, why do we still see such exclusionary trends? I believe it is not enough to just allow access to education but the kind of education received warrants attention too. Effort needs to be made to create in citizens, a conscious understanding of the laws and regulations that protect them. They need to be able to look for legal recourse in the event of unfair treatment, whether in their workplace, homes or in society in general. There is some headway made in this area. A Public Interest Litigation (PIL) has been launched against the Kerala State Electricity Board by a tribal member because of the board's plans to construct a dam near her tribal colony in the Western Ghats despite advice against doing so by many including her own community for fear of repercussions.[24]

There also needs to be a renewed consensus between the state and civil society. Such a highly politicised society such as that in Kerala suffers from the 'strangulating effects of the state'.[25] What is now needed is de-politicisation. This is easier said than done considering historical trends and current benefits for party leaders. However, if genuine democratic deepening is the end goal, then policy makers need to make a conscientious effort at moving away from the highly politicised nature of participatory development planning.

---

22 Tamara Nair, 'Capability and Cultural Subjects'.

23 Economic Times. "At 96.2%, Kerala tops literacy rate chart; Andhra Pradesh worst performer." *The Economic Times*. Monday 7 September, 2020. https://economictimes.indiatimes.com/news/politics-and-nation/at-96-2-kerala-tops-literacy-rate-chart-andhra-pradesh-worst-performer-at-66-4/articleshow/77978682.cms.

24 Tamara Nair, 'Decentralization and the Cultural Politics of Natural Resource Management in Kerala, India', *Singapore Journal of Tropical Geography* 35 (2014): 397–411.

25 M.S. John and Jos Chathukulam, 'Building Social Capital through State Initiative: Participatory Planning in Kerala', *Economic and Political Weekly* 37 (2002): 1940.

Such considerations as those set out above would set the necessary preconditions that must drive decentralised sustainable development. In this Kerala has the potential to lead. The state certainly presents the necessary prerequisites to carry out effective democratic deepening. With its active and literate civic society, and leaders that believe in the potential benefits of devolved governance, Kerala can stand as a beacon for other states in India, South Asia and the developing world. Despite the focus on Kerala, much can be gleaned about decentralised governance and participatory development as presented here.

The much admired Kerala development experience notwithstanding, this discussion has provided some provisional 'truths' that reveal how decentralised governance does not always benefit excluded groups and can in some cases symbolise an exercise of power over disadvantaged communities. These lessons signal the need for caution in embarking on participatory programmes and to ensure that individual and community freedoms are intact. Critics of decentralised governance and greater public participation in development focus on the technical limitations of the approach and emphasise the need for a review of methods.[26] Much of this criticism tends to be mired in naïve understandings of local power structures and levels of subjugation that function within societies, more so when disadvantaged groups are concerned. The need to examine cultural contexts and power dynamics within which decentralisation takes place becomes imperative when we still witness, despite well-meaning attempts at democratic deepening, the disenfranchisement of groups within participatory development mechanisms around the world. This is an essential part of enquiry and I believe the future of all citizens, these communities, and ultimately sustainable development, is dependent upon it.

Bibliography

Agrawal, Arun, and Clark C. Gibson. 'Enchantment and Disenchantment: The Role of Community in Natural Resource Conservation'. *World Development* 27.4 (1999): 629–649.

Chathukulam, Jos, and M. S. John. "Empowerment of Women Panchayat Members: Learning From Kerala (India)." *Asian Journal of Women's Studies* 6.4 (2000): 66–101.

26 Bill Cooke and Uma Kothari, 'The Case for Participation as Tyranny', *Participation: The New Tyranny?*, ed. Bill Cooke and Uma Kothari (London, New York: Zed Books, 2001).

Cooke, Bill, and Uma Kothari. 'The Case for Participation as Tyranny'. *Participation: The New Tyranny?,* edited by Bill Cooke and Uma Kothari, 1–15. London, New York: Zed Books, 2001.

Damodaran, A. 'Tribals, Forests and Resource Conflicts in Kerala, India: The Status Quo of Policy Change'. *Oxford Development Studies* 34.3 (2006): 357–371.

Foucault, Michel. *History of Sexuality*. Victoria, Australia; Penguin Group, 2008.

Jafar, K. "Reservation and Women's Political Freedom: Candidates' Experience From Three Gram Panchayats in Kerala, India." *Social Change* 43.1 (2013): 79–97.

John, M.S, and Jos Chathukulam. 'Building Social Capital through State Initiative: Participatory Planning in Kerala'. *Economic and Political Weekly* 37.20 (2002): 1939–1948.

Kannan, K. P. "Kerala's Turnaround in Growth: Role of Social Development, Remittances and Reform." *Economic and Political Weekly* (2005): 548–554.

Kurien, John. 'The Kerala Model: Its Central Tendency and the "Outlier" '. *Kerala: The Development Experience. Reflections on Sustainability and Replicability*, edited by Govindan Parayil, 178–197. London and New York: Zed Books, 2000.

Lele, Medha, K. 'Local Government: Conflict of Interests and Issues of Legitimisation', *Economic and Political Weekly* 36.51 (2001): 4702–4704.

Menon, Nivedita. 'Sexuality, Caste, Governmentality: Contests over "Gender" in India'. *Feminist Review* 91.1 (2009): 94–112.

Molyneux, Maxine, and Shahrah Razavi. 'Introduction'. *Gender Justice, Development and Rights*, edited by Maxine Molyneux and Shahrah Razavi, 1–42. Oxford: Oxford University Press, 2002.

Nair, Tamara. 'Decentralization and the Cultural Politics of Natural Resource Management in Kerala, India'. *Singapore Journal of Tropical Geography* 35.3 (2014): 397–411.

Nair, Tamara. 'Capability and Cultural Subjects: A Reassessment of Power and Social Development in Kerala, India'. PhD Dissertation, University of New South Wales, 2012.

Navaneeth, M.S. "Reservations for Women in Kerala's Local Self-government Institutions: A Mere Tokenism?" *Working Paper,* Department of Humanities and Social Sciences, IIT Madras (16 May 2020). https://ssrn.com/abstract=3758947.

Omvedt, Gail. 'Kerala Is Part of India: The Kerala Model of Development, Dalits and Globalisation'. *Kerala: The Paradoxes of Public Action and Development*, edited by Joseph Tharamangalam, 188–214. New Delhi: Orient Longman, 2006.

Oommen, M. A. *Rethinking Development: Kerala's Development Experience*. Vol. 2. New Delhi: Concept publishing company, 1999.

Parayil, Govindan, and T. T. Sreekumar. "Kerala's Experience of Development and Change." *Journal of Contemporary Asia* 33.4 (2003): 465–492.

Saradamoni, K. 'Women and the Changed Family in Kerala: Some Masked Realities'. *Kerala: The Paradoxes of Public Action and Development*, edited by Joseph Tharamangalam. New Delhi: Orient Longman, 2006.

Sen, Amartya. *Development as Freedom*. New York: Alfred A. Knopf Inc., 2009.

Stewart, Frances. 'Development and Security'. *Conflict, Security & Development* 4.3 (2004): 261–288.

Tharamangalam, Joseph. 'Understanding Kerala's Paradoxes: The Problematic of the Kerala Model of Development'. *Kerala: The Paradoxes of Public Action and Development,* edited by Joseph Tharamangalam, 1–37. New Delhi: Orient Longman, 2006.

Véron, René. "The "new" Kerala model: Lessons for sustainable development." *World Development* 29.4 (2001): 601–617.

World Commission on Environment and Development, *Our Common Future*. New York: New York Oxford University Press, 1987.

Inventing Citizenship

Lana Zdravković

Abstract

The concept of citizenship is in itself contradictory and exclusive since the process of its nationalization, when it lost its political potential. The nation-state, with all its elements, reduces citizenship into membership of a national community, to the exclusion of all the others. Such a concept has thus failed to establish a political subject. I believe that we need to think of citizenship as a political concept as defined by H. Arendt, É. Balibar, J. Habermas and others. We need to think about citizenship as acting in the public sphere, as *vita activa* which refers to citizenship as thinking and acting as a public rather than a private matter, with an ear for the world and is the responsibility towards future generations which inherit the state of the world. In this way, practising citizenship is not a private activity of maximization of happiness but engagement on the foundations of care for all (Arendt). The politics of citizenship is in a communicative engagement of active people working in the public deliberation (Habermas). We need to invent a new concept of citizenship where modes of belonging are founded on the development of citizenship, and not vice versa (Balibar). This includes the right of entry and residence, work, education, political participation in any country for everyone, not as (neo)liberal principle of 'free choice' but as real dissemination and respect for human rights, which requires the rebalancing of the rights of all citizens, co-living in a particular country (community). Thus it represents a fundamental ethical requirement for radical political equality. This designates citizenship as a process, practice and activity rather than a concluded form. It is always in the making.

Keywords

citizenship – radical equality – emancipation

The European Union (EU) citizenship is in itself an ambivalent and exclusive concept. According to the Maastricht Treaty, it includes only those who already possess the nationality of one of the EU-28. However, more than 20 million citizens of non-EU countries live legally in the EU, and at least 10 million are so called undocumented migrants. These people, many stemming from one or more generations, are indispensable for global prosperity, culture and

© KONINKLIJKE BRILL NV, LEIDEN, 2022 | DOI:10.1163/9789004429253_011

civility of Europe, but are *de facto* second-class citizens in the service of 'full-fledged Europeans'. Such a concept is not a political one if we accept that politics implies recognition of equal individuals in a political community, where equality is not created on the principle of exclusion/sacrifice of the minority in favour of the majority. Equality among EU members, therefore, should be understood in juxtaposition with the inequality of non-members. In my view the citizenship of the future should be thought of not as a contractual or status-oriented relation, but as a political notion, as an action and participation in discussion about public/common matters as determined by Étienne Balibar, Hannah Arendt, Jürgen Habermas, Engin Isin, Iris Marion Young and Nira Yuval-Davis.

1 The Exclusivity of the Concept of Citizenship

The difficulty is the exclusivity of the concept of citizenship as such, even though it has risen from an emancipatory idea (Declaration of the Rights of Man and of the Citizen, 1789). But, at least since Thomas Humphrey Marshall's liberal triad of political, civil and social rights,[1] the concept of citizenship has been nationalised, so it has been losing its political potential; it is constructed through affiliation to a particular nation-state and is applied only to its members as a set of rights, being equalised with the nationality that has already been equalised with ethnicity and/or race. This generates the state as a national community that functions on exclusion as a rule. Liberal policies (of care, tolerance, multiculturalism etc.) are justified as based on practices of inclusion of marginalised ones, yet they never touch the true reasons of inequality, but rather leave them unchanged. The state as nation-state with its concepts of nation and national identity, defined by ethnical, historical and cultural presumptions such as loyalty, borders and sovereignty 'devour' the idea of political community. The citizenship is therefore reduced to the membership in a national community, which generates the exclusion based on separation between the 'true' and 'false' members(hip). This transforms the citizenship into a privilege, an honour, a surplus of rights. Inclusion into such a privileged group is selective and arbitrary (*ius soli, ius sanguinis*), while the contracting rules could never be influenced by the foreigner: 'once a migrant,

1 Marshall, Thomas Humphrey, *Citizenship and Social Class: And Other Essays* (Cambridge: University Press, 1950).

always a migrant'. Such a concept of citizenship fails to establish a political community and political subject.

Étienne Balibar names this concept 'constructing of fictive ethnicity',[2] to explain the way of generating societies and peoples to be established in a system of nation-states with a historical perspective, and, to clarify how that tendentious nationalisation of societies and peoples, ergo cultures, languages and genealogies, influences its own representation and ways of giving meanings to its own 'identities', from its core.[3] Therefore, he uses the term to mark 'the societies constructed by the nation-state'.[4] In this manner, he shows the split of the term 'people' into two complementary terms coined by the tradition of political philosophy: the Greek word *ethos,* meaning people as an imaginary community of loyalty and kinship, and *demos,* which defines people as a collective subject of representation, decision-making and rights.[5]

For these purposes, the state needs specific structural and/or symbolic violence known under various names: 'assimilation', 'integration', 'naturalisation', 'adaptation', 'melting pot' ... Its purpose is to equalise differences between groups in a way of adjusting 'minorities' to 'majority'. The violence is institutionalised and spontaneous, visible and invisible, structured and unstructured at the same time. It is most successfully carried out by school and family, but also by other Althusserian ideological apparatuses of the state (legal, political, trade-unionist, information, cultural, religious etc.),[6] or the very set of state's tools that Foucault names 'discipline'.[7] As history shows, two more elements are very important in this process of ultimate normalisation, which is the reconstruction of various primary identities into one collective, universal national identity: language and race. Both express the idea that the national character ('spirit' or 'substance') is inseparable from the people, and is therefore immanent to them.

When individuals are constructed as united fictive ethnicities against a social environment of universalist representation that is inherent to every individual, and the people is separated to different ethnic groups that potentially

2 Étienne Balibar and Immanuel Wallerstein, *Race, Nation, Class: Ambiguous Identities* (London: Verso, 1991), 96.

3 Ibid.

4 Ibid.

5 In that context Immanuel Wallerstein speaks about 'the construction of peoplehood', cf. Ibid., 71.

6 Althusser, Louis. 'Ideology and Ideological State Apparatuses' in *Lenin and Philosophy and Other Essays*. (Monthly Review Press, 1971).

7 Foucault, Michel. *Discipline and Punish: the Birth of the Prison*. (New York: Random House, 1975).

match the same number of nations, then the national ideology is at its peak; it is not only a specific state's strategy of population control, but by also generating demands and wishes, initiatives and needs of that population, it becomes biopolitics *par excellence*.[8] It is clear that in the creation of a nation, national-affiliation awareness and formation of national identity, is in fact an illusion and a convincing one at that. Being created and sustained through national institutions and ideology, it is a fabrication. It is based on belief that the generations, following one another in that particular territory through centuries, create an unchangeable essence or substance, and that that process of development, of which we are a culmination, was the only possible and fatal one. Therefore we can conclude that, under certain conditions, only imaginary (imagined) communities are real.[9]

2 National Unification as Generic Ideology of a Nation-State

Indeed, those who 'fight nationalism' within such a constructed socio-political model of nation-state overlook the important fact that nationalism is a generic organic ideology of every nation-state, which does not mean that all nationalisms are state-based, neither that the nation-state functions on the basis of nationalism only. Nationalism is inscribed in the core of nation being realised in a form of nation-state, which confers status of national affiliation or citizenship, based on the principle of exclusion, of visible and invisible borders, materialised in laws and regulations or constructed in our minds.

Great equalisation between citizenship and nationality, introduced in the name of sovereignty of the modern states, therefore acts against its democratic meaning. The basic problem is that not only the national affiliation (as a cultural category), but also the citizenship (as an administrative category) emerge as an individual's essence.

8 In other place Étienne Balibar introduce the term 'homo nationalis', cf. Étienne Balibar, *Mi, državljani Evrope?: meje, država, ljudstvo/We, the People of Europe?: Borders, State, Peoplehood* (Ljubljana: Založba Sophia, 2007), 21.

9 Benedict Anderson stresses that the socially constructed character of ethnical communities lies in the foundation of the idea of the nation as imaginary political community. Anderson also analyses nationalism as a product of the phenomenon of imaginary communities and by that significantly justifies the constructivist theory of nation: 'nationalism is not the awakening of the nations and their self-esteem: nationalism rather *invents* nations at the places where they are absent'. Cf. Benedict Anderson, *Imagined Communities: Reflections on the Origin and Spread of Nationalism* (London: Verso, 1991), 15.

This leads to differentiation between universal human rights and social, economic, cultural, i.e. political rights in a state. On one hand, we have universal human rights defined by 'transnational' Universal Declaration of Human Rights (1948), the successor of famous Declaration of the Rights of Man and of the Citizen (1789), and on the other hand, it is limited by the sovereign nation-state, because the Declaration is not an obligatory document. In that way, universal human rights that include rights to education, work, health and social protection, political expression, the right to emigrate and immigrate or right of free movement, valid for all and always on a declarative level, are in fact always profiled through particular national belonging and legislation.

> Contemporary concept of citizenship – that operates through institutions of sovereign nation-state that are in function of managing universal by subordinating subjects – therefore goes together with an extensive system of social exclusion, appearing as normalisation and socialisation of anthropological differences.[10]

Understanding the attitude toward non-citizens is therefore a key to understanding citizenship. As humankind, since the French revolution, has assumed an image of 'family of nations', the image of a human being, as a consequence of that, is not an individual, but rather a projected image of a nation; for that reason, the impossibility of realisation of 'universality' of human rights is radically revealed exactly in the cases of persons who do not have status of citizen of a sovereign (national) state, or, who have lost support and protection of their governments. As shown by Hannah Arendt, the paradox and difficulty of this concept lies in the fact that the loss of all human rights matches the very moment when a person becomes 'just' a human being, without any other political and social attributes.[11]

---

10 Balibar, *Mi, državljani Evrope?: meje, država, ljudstvo/We, the People of Europe?: Borders, State, Peoplehood*, 79–80.

11 Hannah Arendt, *The Origins of Totalitarianism* (New York: Harcourt Brace and Co., 1978), 383. The natural 'bare life' therefore appears incompatible with the legal order of the nation-state: people without state or citizenship are people without existence. The same principle is currently applied in cases of migrants, asylum seekers, refugees (officially called 'illegal migrants') and *sans-papiers*; in Slovenia, for instance, the Erased. The erased residents of the Republic of Slovenia are the individuals who used to be citizens of the former common state of Yugoslavia that Slovenia used to be a part of, and at the same time of one of Yugoslavia's six republics, and who, for various subjective or objective reasons, did not apply for citizenship of the new state of Slovenia in 1991, or they were refused after applying for it. These individuals consequently became subjects of the Act on Foreigners. Although they *already had legally confirmed status of permanent residence*

The loss of citizenship's rights *de facto* means the loss of human rights. A refugee, a migrant or a person without citizenship, the one who should be a subject of human rights *par excellence* (Giorgio Agamben's *homo sacer*),'[12] as they are the only ones left to refer to, in fact reveals a radical crisis of that term. As stressed by Arendt, such a person has no place in the world to be, as being erased from the order of politics is akin to being erased from the norm of humanity.[13]

That condition, as shown by Étienne Balibar, is the result of colonial heritage: the colonial subject is a 'citizen by birth', whilst the immigrant worker is not (there is a significant word for immigrant in the Anglo-American vocabulary: *alien*); although more or less integrated in society and partly included in its system of rights and obligations, one can hardly get out from the minority status. So today we are facing the process of 're-colonisation of social conditions' that started in the 1980s as a consequence of economic globalisation and new inequality, both on a local (national) and global level. For this transnational phenomenon of 'racism without races', Étienne Balibar introduces the term 'meta-racism' or 'neo-racism'.[14] It is characterised by two features: the

in Slovenia, and only because they could not or did not want to ask for the *citizenship* of a new-born state they were, without relevant legal basis, overnight and without any notice or warning, erased from the Registry of Permanent Residents (on 26th February 1992). By that act, more than 25 600 persons (more than 1% of Slovenia's population in that time) lost the legal foundation of existence, as they were robbed of all the rights related to the status of permanent residence (work permit, social rights, health insurance, the right to housing etc.).

12 Agamben borrows the concept of *homo sacer* or 'the bare life' from Walter Benjamin, setting it as a crystallisation point of mutation of modern politics. He understands it as a continuation and radicalisation of Foucault's thesis on biopolitics. Developing the idea of a new character of sovereign power that puts itself on a position of deciding on life outside any law, Agamben borrows Carl Schmitt's idea of the state of exception to describe the hidden intersection between *zoe* and *bios*, or, 'between juridical-institutional and biopolitical model of power'. Cf. Giorgio Agamben, *Homo Sacer: Sovereign Power and Bare Life* (Stanford: Stanford University Press, 1998), 14. *Homo sacer* though does not represent a simple exclusion, but a hierarchical inclusion – an inclusion through exclusion.

13 Although both Arendt and Agamben highlight the visibility of 'the bare life' in the field of politics, however, their conclusions are radically different. While Arendt stresses the classical opposition between public (political) and private life, Agamben emphasizes the situation of modern democracy, based on a mix of those two lives, more exactly on a reduction of *bios* to bare *zoe*. Although Arendt also sees a radical novelty in the intrusion of biological life into the political scene, she interprets it, unlike Agamben, as a sign of decadence of political living in modern democracies and not as a paradigm of the modern power based on a state of exception. In that sense, Arendt puts the idea of democracy opposite to totalitarianism, while Agamben supposes an inner solidarity between democracy and totalitarianism.

14 Balibar and Wallerstein, *Race, Nation, Class: Ambiguous Identities*, 17.

place of race or biological heredity has been taken by the terms ethnicity, culture and invincibility of cultural differences; the transition from the notion of colonialism to the notion of immigration.

3 Opening the Borders of Citizenship

I believe, according to Hannah Arendt, that the concept of citizenship has to be rethought as an operation in the public sphere, as *vita activa*: the citizenship refers to thinking and acting as public, not as private concern; it means being sensitive to the world and acting responsibly for future generations who will inherit its condition. In that sense, the practising of the citizenship is not a private activity of maximising of happiness (already forced by the (neo)liberal principle), but an engagement based on concern for all. Ethics of citizenship therefore requires common answers to common matters, arising from sameness (alikeness) and not otherness (differences) between individuals.[15]

As Étienne Balibar claims, to construct 'the citizenship in the world' means to enable rights and act in the world as a political community.[16] It means to invent the concept of citizenship wherein the modes of belonging are founded on the development of it, not vice versa (Étienne Balibars's concepts *droit de cité* and 'constitution of citizenship' (*politeia*)).[17] More precisely, that means liberated, expanded right to enter and stay, also right to work, education, political engagement and so forth, in any state; i.e. the right to equal political rights for all inhabitants, regardless of their nationality, on a local, national and community level. However, that it is not about the (neo)liberal principle of 'free choice', but about the true widening and respecting of human rights, that requires actual equalising of rights of all inhabitants co-living in certain state (community), and therefore constitutes a genuine ethical request for radical political equality. Such de-substantialisation of citizenship announces that the citizenship is a process, practice, activity of a citizen – not a concluded form. It is always

15 Cf. Hannah Arendt, *Vita Activa* (Ljubljana: Krtina, 1996).

16 Otherwise we are facing 'citizenship without community', cf. Balibar, *Mi, državljani Evrope?: meje, država, ljudstvo/We, the People of Europe?: Borders, State, Peoplehood*, 70. This opens the important question of what the concept of community actually means in the time of crisis of nation-states.

17 Balibar, *Mi, državljani Evrope?: meje, država, ljudstvo/ We, the People of Europe?: Borders, State, Peoplehood*, 65.

> in progress, dependent on the activity of all, a set of practices that connect both poles, the attitude toward oneself and toward others (cooperation, recognition, solidarity), and so it is a process of constant inventing.[18]

The concept of 'democratisation of borders'[19] should be understood in the same context as borders are, currently and more than ever before, labels for sovereignty; borders are a non-democratic condition of democracy that operates mainly as a security control, social segregation, non-equal access to resources for quality life, even as an institutional distribution of livelihood and death and a basis for institutional violence. For a rich man from a rich state, a member of the 'dominant nation',[20] not to mention members of 'international bourgeois',[21] the crossing of a border became a formality, a place of symbolic recognition of his social status. But for a poor resident of a poor state, a member of the 'inferior' or criminalised nation, asylum or job seeker, the border crossing is not a right, but rather a privilege. It is not only an obstacle hard to overcome, but also a place of repeatedly colliding, across which she/he goes again and again; after all it is a place of living. It is an upsetting 'space-time zone, almost a habitat'.[22] However, Étienne Balibar's demand does not mean a simple cancellation or abolition of borders, but particularly multilateral, mediated control of their operation by inhabitants; Étienne Balibar thus demands efficient 'de-fetishisation'[23] or 'de-sacralisation'[24] both of visible (physical) and invisible (symbolic) borders. For him, democratisation of institution of border means 'using it in favour of the people and subordinate it to their collective supervision',[25] as 'natural borders – the big myth of foreign policy of nation-states – does not exist and have never existed'.[26]

That actually means unifying of human and citizen's rights, as citizenship should be again and again identified in dialectics of conflicts and solidarity, as a responsibility and active/activist operation. Étienne Balibar also names that

18 Ibid., 159.
19 Ibid., 132–133.
20 Ibid., 61.
21 Ibid.
22 Étienne Balibar, 'Is a Philosophy of Human Civic Rights Possible? New Reflections on Equaliberty', *The South Atlantic Quarterly* CIII.2–3 (2004), 406.
23 Balibar, *Mi, državljani Evrope?: meje, država, ljudstvo/ We, the People of Europe?: Borders, State, Peoplehood*, 133.
24 Ibid., 137.
25 Ibid., 132.
26 Ibid.

demand 'cosmopolitization of human rights',[27] where citizenship and society are correlated in a completely new context.

We have to recognize the real concept of human rights as a conflictual one, as it always refers to postulates of democracy, but at the same time puts into question its existence.[28] Consequently, it cannot be established without internal unification of concepts of rights of 'human and citizen', which is a 'radical discursive procedure that deconstructs and reconstructs the politics'.[29] It starts by pushing the democracy to reach its limits, where it leaves the field of institutional policy, but only in order to immediately show that the human rights as such are not real, and have no value if not settled as unlimited political right of all to have a citizenship.

4 Inventing Citizenship

The emancipatory aspiration which, as Étienne Balibar claims, does not happen spontaneously, but always by struggles of 'different categories' of people – Jacques Rancière's 'uncountable' or 'part of those who have no part'[30] – raises a specific universalism: if people are free (political institution must consider them as such), it is because they are equal, and if they are equal (they should be recognised as such), it is because they are free.[31] And this is also the crucial point of Hannah Arendt's concept of 'rights to have rights'.[32] When such a maxim is written into a political and social reality, its direct result is that exclusion from the citizenship (in the first place from the 'active' citizenship, typical by full exercising of political rights) cannot be interpreted and justified in any way other than as the actual exclusion from humanity or human norm.

Understanding the concept of citizenship as an unconditional access to the fundamental equality is crucial, as it articulates the relation between individual and collective. Étienne Balibar insists that it is enough to be a human (without attributes) in order to be a citizen (a subject of politics). The struggle

27 Ibid.

28 Étienne Balibar, *Masses, Classes, Ideas: Studies on Politics and Philosophy Before and After Marx* (New York, London: Routledge, 1994), 205–226.

29 Ibid., 212.

30 Cf. Jacques Rancière, *Disagreement* (Minneapolis: University of Minnesota Press, 1999).

31 This is the core of Balibar's concept of 'equaliberty', cf. Balibar, *Mi, državljani Evrope?: meje, država, ljudstvo/We, the People of Europe?: Borders, State, Peoplehood*, 78.

32 Arendt, Hannah. *Vita Activa*. Ljubljana: Krtina, 1996.

against the denial of citizenship is therefore the life of emancipatory politics.[33] This concept of radical democracy

> exceeds far beyond the simple theme of "accepting the Foreign" (not to mention levels that start with inclusion and integration, but finish with assimilation). Because *everybody*, including "indigenous", must at least symbolically pledge their citizenship's identity that was obtained or inherited from the past, and *reconstruct it in the present* along with all others: with those who currently share the same "destiny" on a strip of the Earth, regardless of where they come from, how long they remain at a place, and irrespective of "legitimacy". That does not mean that the past does not exist or that it is of no use, but that it is not a heritage, that it does not provide a right of firstborn. That means that there are no "first residents" of a civic territory.[34]

It is clear that the aim of the 'policies of immigration control' or 'migration management' is not an ending of so called illegal employment and immigration, neither of illegal labour trafficking which supplies that employment, nor the illegal conditions resulting therefrom. On the contrary, it is rather about 'the reproduction of illegality that indirectly justifies the urge of repressive measures'.[35] It is about producing illegality in advance to later make it the reason for existence of security apparatus that causes 'syndrome of insecurity', which affects the whole state. Consequently, the rebellions, struggles and demands for active political participation performed exactly by non-citizens themselves are, for Étienne Balibar, a paradigm of living of the emancipatory politics.[36] In our attempt to re-invent citizenship we must, therefore, critically re-think the question of constitution of the people that goes along with constitution of the state. After critically re-questioning that ideology, we will, hopefully, be able

---

33 Balibar, 'Is a Philosophy of Human Civic Rights Possible?', 15–17.

34 Balibar, *Mi, državljani Evrope?: meje, država, ljudstvo/ We, the People of Europe?: Borders, State, Peoplehood*, 161.

35 Ibid. 82.

36 That notion is confirmed by various movements that demand universality of life and being through struggle for access to citizenship for all. The movements devoted more of their attention and networking efforts to that subject in the time of global demonstrations against the governance of capitalist elites and fortifications of financial capital (IMF, World Bank, WTO), especially since Seattle 1999. Some of the key movements in this respect are *Global Project* and *Ya basta!* in Italy, *No one is illegal* in various countries, *Sans-papier* in France, *Dostje!* and later *Nevidni delavci sveta* (*Invisible Workers of the World* (*IWW*)) in Slovenia.

to think about the constructing of the community not founded as a national/ identitarian one, but as a political one, hence assuming radical equality of whoever with whomever.

Bibliography

Agamben, Giorgio. Homo Sacer: Sovereign Power and Bare Life. Stanford: Stanford University Press, 1998.

Althusser, Louis. 'Ideology and Ideological State Apparatuses' in Lenin and Philosophy and Other Essays. Monthly Review Press, 1971.

Althusser, Louis and Étienne Balibar. Reading Capital. London: Verso, 2009.

Anderson, Benedict. Imagined Communities: Reflections on the Origin and Spread of Nationalism. London: Verso, 1991.

Arendt, Hannah. The Origins of Totalitarianism. New York: Harcourt Brace and Co., 1978.

Arendt, Hannah. Vita Activa. Ljubljana: Krtina, 1996.

Balibar, Étienne. 'Citizen Subject'. Who Comes After the Subject?, edited by Jean-LucNancy, 33–57. New York, London: Routledge, 1991.

Balibar, Étienne and Immanuel Wallerstein. Race, Nation, Class: Ambiguous Identities. London: Verso, 1991a.

Balibar, Étienne. Masses, Classes, Ideas: Studies on Politics and Philosophy Before and After Marx. New York, London: Routledge, 1994.

Balibar, Étienne. 'Culture and Identity (Working Notes)'. Identity in Question, edited by John Rajchman, 173–199. New York, London: Routledge, 1995.

Balibar, Étienne. 'Is a Philosophy of Human Civic Rights Possible? New Reflections on Equaliberty'. The South Atlantic Quarterly CIII.2–3 (2004): 311–322.

Balibar, Étienne. Mi, državljani Evrope?: meje, država, ljudstvo/ We, the People of Europe?: Borders, State, Peoplehood. Ljubljana: Založba Sophia, 2007.

Beznec, Barbara, ed. 'Once upon an Erasure: From Citizens to Illegal Residents in the Republic of Slovenia'. Časopis za kritiko znanosti, domišljijo in novo antropologijo, XXXVI.228 (2007).

Dedić, Jasminka, Vlasta Jalušič and Jelka Zorn. The Erased: Organised Innocence and the Politics of Exclusion. Ljubljana: Peace Institute, 2003.

Foucault, Michel. Discipline and Punish: the Birth of the Prison. New York: Random House, 1975.

Foucault, Michel. The Birth of Biopolitics: Lectures at the Collège de France, 1978–1979. London, New York: Palgrave Macmillan, 2010.

Kogovšek, Neža, Jelka Zorn, Sara Pistotnik, Uršula Lipovec Čebron, Veronika Bajt, Brankica Petković and Lana Zdravković. The Scars of the Erasure. Ljubljana: Peace Institute, 2010.

Marshall, Thomas Humphrey. Citizenship and Social Class: And Other Essays. Cambridge: University Press, 1950.

Mezzadra, Sandro. 'Državljanstvo v gibanju'/ 'Citizenship in the Motion'. Časopis za kritiko znanosti, domišljijo in novo antropologijo XXXII.217–218 (2004): 59–66.

Mezzadra, Sandro. 'Border as Method, or the Multiplication of Labor'. European Institute for Progressive Cultural Policies, 15 September 2012. Viewed 5 October 2015. http://eipcp.net/transversal/0608/mezzadraneilson/en.

Rancière, Jacques. 'Politics, Identification and Subjectivization'. Identity in Question, edited by John Rajhcman, 63–73. New York, London: Routledge, 1995.

Rancière, Jacques. Disagreement. Minneapolis: University of Minnesota Press, 1999.

Rancière, Jacques. 'Who Is the Subject of the Rights of Man?'. South Atlantic Quarterly CIII.2–3 (2004): 297–310.

Zdravković, Lana. 'Paradoks koncepta človekovih pravic in boj zoper odrekanja državljanstva kot življenjske emancipacijske politike: primer Izbrisanih prebivalcev Slovenije'/ 'The Paradox of the Concepts of Human Rights and the Struggle against Citizenship Rejection as Life Emancipatory Politics: The Case of the Erased Inhabitants of Slovenia'. Časopis za kritiko znanosti, domišljijo in novo antropologijo XXXVII.235–236 (2009): 289–294.

Zdravković, Lana. 'The Struggle against the Denial of Citizenship as a Paradigm of Emancipatory Politics'. The Scars of the Erasure: a Contribution to the Critical Understanding of the Erasure of People from the Register of Permanent Residents of the Republic of Slovenia, edited by Neža Kogovšek Šalamun, Veronika Bajt, Brankica Petković, Uršula Lipovec Čebron, Sara Pistotnik, Jelka Zorn and Lana Zdravković, 257–277. Ljubljana: Peace Institute, 2010.

Zdravković, Lana. 'Emancipatory Politics as a Process of Involving "Wrong" Names'. The Renaming Machine, edited by Suzana Milevska, 72–79. Ljubljana: Zavod P.A.R.A.S.I.T.E., 2010.

Zdravković, Lana. 'An Arche or Barbarism: The Responsibility of Being of/in the World'. Journal of Visual Arts Practice X.2 (2011): 113–123.

Zdravković, Lana. 'Misliti nemogoče: onkraj predstavništva'/ 'To Think the Impossible: Beyond the Principle of Representation'. Časopis za kritiko znanosti, domišljijo in novo antropologijo XLII.257 (2014): 53–66.

Index

www.ingramcontent.com/pod-product-compliance
Lightning Source LLC
Chambersburg PA
CBHW031327230926
51848CB00001B/128
9789004429246